The
No
Bullsht
Guide
To A
Happier Life

The No Bullsh*t Guide

To A
Happier Life

By Helen Calvert

Clear Day Publications

ISBN: 978-1-7396134-0-2 (paperback)
        978-1-7396134-2-6 (paperback - A5 format)
        978-1-7396134-1-9 (ebook)

Published by:
Clear Day Publications

Cover design:
Victoria Murray, VCM Graphic Design

Page layout and production:
Catherine Williams, Chapter One Book Production

Bless the largeness inside me, no matter how I fear it... When I am dust, sing these words over my bones: she was a voice.

Sue Monk Kidd

This book is dedicated to everyone who has blessed the largeness in me, and to all who have helped me to be a voice.

CONTENTS

PREFACE

This is your no bullshit guide to a happier life. Quick, but not necessarily easy, tips to help you to squeeze every last drop of enjoyment out of your business and your life.

This book is geared towards people like me who are the decision makers in their working life – business owners and freelancers. I hope, though, that it will also provide helpful insights for everyone, no matter their employment status.

My mission is to enjoy life to its fullest. We are here for as long as we get, we have plenty of challenges along the way, so if I see an opportunity to enjoy myself, to enjoy life, I am going to take it, and I hope that I can help you to make that your mission too. The down times are awful, and we have to navigate our way through them, so we do not want to miss out on the up times, and we can create many, many up times for ourselves.

I do not believe in the 3-step wonder programme to success. I do believe that there are loads of things that we can do to make our lives happier, but I am not necessarily going to be talking about things that are easy. If you are after an easy ride, this book may not be for you, but I believe we are all big enough and old enough to understand that for the things we want, we have to put in the work. It's just knowing what that work is and how we can do it.

I am a coach, a business owner, a parent to two boys. I am a girlfriend and an ex-wife, and I have my own mental health challenges. I come at life from the point of view of an anxious person, and if I was unmedicated and had not had any talking therapy, I would be a basket case, and indeed I was in my twenties! My boys have special educational needs and one of them was born with a congenital heart defect. My boyfriend lives 4,000 miles away, in America. So, like you, I have my challenges, which are there to make life interesting!

I am delighted that you have picked up this book and are here for some no bullshit talk about the things that we all face and navigate.

Ready to go? Let's do this...

INTRODUCTION

A listener to my podcast once wrote of it 'the honest approach to being an unapologetic version of yourself is brilliant'.

Sometimes you get feedback that just makes your heart sing. I have spent forty years learning how to be an unapologetic version of myself, and being able to bring some of that to other people is just wonderful.

We all have life experiences and viewpoints that make our advice valuable, so, really, my qualification for writing this book is that I am a human being just like you, and I have some insights you may find useful. Still, it is nice to understand where an author fits into the world, so I can tell you that I am a qualified life coach who also runs an agency of virtual assistants called Clear Day. I have been running my own business since 2018, and I have been a parent since 2011. Further back, I have been a human female since 1980. All of those things have taught me a hell of a lot.

I have spent over ten years on social media being part of supportive communities, at first for parenting and then for business owners. I have also, alongside that, been on my own journey of counselling, therapy and coaching which, in part, led me to become a coach. My other reason for training as a coach was that, as a virtual assistant, I was working with many business owners who didn't have anyone to talk to about their fears and aspirations. I enjoyed being that person for them and wanted to learn how to do it really effectively.

All of those experiences have led me to the conclusion that having a fulfilling and happy life is not complicated, but neither is it easy. The search for that is peppered with a certain amount of bullshit along the way. In 2021, I launched my podcast, *The No Bullsh*t Guide To A Happier Life*, which I wanted to be a place where I could discuss some of my learnings, opinions and questions about what we are all trying to achieve, and how we go about that. The podcast has been very successful; I have been delighted with it and enjoyed it, and I have had some wonderful feedback. The logical next step was, therefore, to pull together the podcast and some of my other content and some more of my musings into a book, so you can access what is, hopefully, a coherent narrative about the ways in which we can help ourselves to get to where we want to be.

A couple of definitions would be useful here. Firstly, what do I mean by 'happy'? Happy is an extremely nebulous and subjective term, and it encompasses a number of different experiences. In this context, what I mean by happy is having the capacity to feel joy and experiencing joy on a fairly regular basis, having the capacity to feel peace and contentment and experiencing that on a fairly regular basis, and feeling fulfilled in our lives. To me, happiness is feeling as though we have left it all out on the field, and at the end of our lives we will not have regrets about the things that we did not try. Happiness is being true to ourselves and not abandoning our true selves in the hope of being acceptable to others. It is a big term and the pursuit of happiness is a lifelong journey.

What do I mean by bullshit? There are many people who imagine they have found the answer to how we can reach happiness in its full definition as I have just outlined it, and they will try to tell you, or usually sell you, an answer that is quite limited. For me, it is not possible that there is one activity, hobby, way of living, way of being that can achieve all of that happiness for us if we just do that one thing. Humans and life are way more complicated than that, and imagining if we just do six months of yoga or try open water swimming or try a low-carb diet or journal every day, we will then be eternally happy is, to me, bullshit.

The other thing I find suspect is any quick and easy system. You do step one, step two, step three and voilà, magic wand: happiness.

I wanted to be very careful with this book not to give you the impression that living a fulfilling life is easy to achieve, but I did want to give you the impression that the road to it is not a complex one. There are fairly clear things that we can do to make our happiness far more likely, but the trouble is they are not easy. There is a lot of mindset work to be done, by which I mean that we need to look at the stories and rules and beliefs we were given in childhood and earlier in our lives. We need to unpick those, figure out how they are serving us or not, figure out how to change the ones that are not serving us, with what to replace them and how to nurture ourselves through that process.

What on earth does any of this have to do with being a business owner? This book will be useful for anybody who would like to have a happy and fulfilling life, but it is particularly geared towards business owners because they are my people. It is also particularly geared towards women because I am one, and I have had many years of supporting women through their parenting and business challenges. I am confident the content of this book will be helpful to you if you are a female business owner. I am also pretty confident the content of this book will be helpful to you if you are a man in employment, but that will be for you to decide.

I believe that an understanding of our emotional well-being and the things that create our current mindset is vital for being successful in business. Running our own business means showing up pretty much every day, doing a lot of things alone, pushing ourselves out of our comfort zone and making ourselves vulnerable. It also means a lot of hard work and, therefore, having solid boundaries unless we want to run into burnout. None of these things is easy, and they are all made much harder if we are carrying around unhelpful mindset blocks, anxieties and stories.

This book is about digging into how our emotional well-being connects with our success in business and with the way in which we reach our goals.

The values of my business, Clear Day, are calm, clarity, confidence, focus and progress. These are the things I hope this book brings to you. When we start with calm, we are much more able to look things full in the face and get clear about what we perhaps need to change or improve. When we get that clarity, we start to feel confident because, even if there is a lot of work to be done, we know we are on the right path. When we feel confident that we are on the right track, we can focus on the things we need to do to reach our goals, which makes progress so much more likely.

You will find a lot of the chapters have a pop-out box highlighting a 'mindset block'. These are the thought processes that are common to many of us but which can get in the way of our making progress towards a happier life. They are things to notice because once we have an awareness of them we can take steps to reduce the blockage and make gentle changes to our mindset. Keeping a note of the ones which particularly resonate with you would also provide a wonderful starting point for any future discussions you may have with a counsellor, coach, therapist, mentor or friend.

The chapters in this book are in a particular order that makes sense to me, as we start with ways to tackle the most pressing issues for business owners: making sales, staying organised and getting stuff done. Once we are on top of those areas, we move on to think about self-belief, self-worth and self-care, as I believe it is difficult for us to make a great deal more progress without those things being in place. Once we are meeting our needs and valuing ourselves we move back to business to explore leadership, team management and work-life balance – some of the tougher areas of being a business owner. That leads us into the 'life' side of the balance, where I discuss parenting, sex and relationships. Having looked at all aspects of our lives as business owners, we move on to life goals, the big picture, and then to ways of thinking and ways of being that can hold us back from reaching those goals and finding fulfilment. Finally, we end with a discussion of money, bringing us full circle to making sales and building our business, but looking at it with new information about our sense of self and the stories we are holding within us.

The order in which you read the chapters is, however, entirely up to you, and each chapter works as a stand-alone essay. You can dip in and out of topics as they feel interesting and relevant to you. I have also ended most chapters with summary points to help you to identify the key actions or thinking points from each one.

I end every episode of my podcast with an injunction to my listeners to be excessively kind to themselves and to squeeze every last drop of enjoyment out of life. In the coming pages you will learn what I mean by excessive kindness and why it is so vital to our success and happiness. I hope that in reading this book you find new ways to show yourself kindness and love and that this leads to you being able to squeeze every last drop of enjoyment out of your business and your life.

OWNING YOUR OWN STORY

B efore we dive into the business essentials, I will start by talking about stories. Realising we, and everyone around us, are living inside our own story has been an eye-opener for me, and it can help to put certain things into perspective.

As much as we like to think we live in reality, in truth we each live inside our own story. Memory is a tricky thing, often showing us things in a way that isn't quite accurate. The future is a castle we build in the sky, to the point that it is quite possible (and normal) to grieve for the loss of plans that never actually happened. The present moment is filled with worries, desires, things to remember, the jukebox of our brains and all kinds of other noise. Reality? We are barely in it.

That is okay, as long as we recognise that is how it is for us, and for everybody around us. We all need the cushion of our own story to get us through our day. We are the leading characters in our own stories, everything that happens to us we see through the camera lens of our own personal movie. Ever wondered why people behave the way they do and why they make the choices they make? Sometimes it is because those choices fit with the story they are living.

So what does it mean to 'own' our story, and why is that important?

It means recognising the story we are telling ourselves and others, deciding whether it is the story we want to live, and if it is, standing up and saying, 'This is my story, and I am allowed to live it'. This can be something simple, such as, 'I am a creative, joyful, disorganised, spontaneous person, and I love that', rather than living inside somebody else's story about you which might be 'Oh, she's a scatterbrain'. It could be standing up and saying, 'I am happy with my life choices even if they are not the choices the people around me would have made'. Or it could be saying, 'I struggle with certain things because I had a traumatic experience, and I do not need to apologise for that.'

Notice I mentioned living in other people's stories about us. The very first people who tend to tell our story are our parents. Ever catch yourself saying about your kids, 'Oh, she's such an entertainer!' or 'You just know he's going to be trouble'? I do it all the time, even though I try not to. Those are your stories about your children, and if you tell them often enough, they will believe them. The tumultuous transition of the teenage years is in part their opportunity to start to tell and own their own stories, but if the parental stories are too strong (or too unhelpful) that can be a challenge.

What stories are you living in which are actually stories that other people have thrust upon you?

Two years ago when I did a course of NLP coaching, I identified my core values, and one of them is owning my own story. This is incredibly important to me, and other people trying to tell my story for me is really uncomfortable. Owning my own story is a boundary I try to uphold, as I find it distressing to listen to others telling my story back to me and getting it wrong. This is not about 'accuracy' as none of us lives in reality. This is about my right to tell my story the way I want it to be told.

How strongly I feel about this is in part due to the fact that I lived other people's stories of myself for far too long. I now have a very strong sense of my own story and I own it 100 per cent. It is not the story of a good obedient girl or of a vulnerable confused individual. It is the story of a strong and passionate woman who always chooses the path of adventure and joy and freedom.

It is so important we decide what our story is and what we want it to be. Stories are powerful things, and if we don't choose our story, we will end up living somebody else's version of it.

It is also really important to remember that the way people see us is always through the lens of their own story. Are we good or bad, helpful or mean, desirable or off-putting, impressive or ridiculous? There is no 'right' answer to these questions because it depends what part we are playing in someone else's movie.

You cannot play the quirky best friend or the love interest or the mentor or the comedy relief in everybody's movie. In some people's movie you are going to be the annoyance, the obstruction, the nemesis, the cautionary tale. That's okay, that is your place in their credits. All that matters is what you choose for your starring role. You only get one. It is the lead role in your own life, and that role you get to pick for yourself. Let's help you to go out there and be a star.

MY STORY

Having established the importance of our stories, what is mine? What have been the crucial experiences that have led me to where I am today, what has shaped my personal philosophy? Let me give you my potted history...

I am an only child of financially comfortable parents, so my childhood was steeped in privilege. I was a precocious, intelligent, joyful and imaginative child, and a passionate, ambitious, opinionated teenager. Running alongside all of that was a thread of anxiety and fear of abandonment that is a result of multi-generational family trauma and genetic predisposition. So, like everybody else, I had both wonderful times and troublesome experiences and am a product of both nature and nurture.

I started to lose myself when I began to have intimate relationships at age 16. By the time I graduated from university, I was heartbroken, desperate for validation, sexually disconnected from myself and living with anxiety day to day, although I had no idea that was the case.

Enter the man with whom I spent the next 15 years of my life and with whom I had my two beautiful boys, Edward and

David. He was a very safe option, a good man, protective, intelligent, hard-working and caring. Everything that my anxious, lost, frightened self needed, and we built a life together.

I started to have counselling in my mid-twenties and there began the long, long journey back to the joyful, passionate, imaginative and ambitious person I had always been underneath the anxiety. That journey has so far taken in the following stops and sights along the way:

* counselling
* CBT
* postnatal anxiety
* anti-anxiety medication
* analysis with a psychiatrist
* NLP coaching.

All of this has been possible due to my financial privilege because all of that treatment was paid for privately.

Alongside that journey was the public journey that other people could see:

* a career as a secretary/receptionist, financial services administrator then marketing executive in professional services firms in Manchester
* marriage
* motherhood
* a career break for parenting purposes, during which time I did a lot of voluntary parent support and campaigning in the perinatal arena.

I was slowly working my way back to myself by the time I fell pregnant with David, and then his arrival accelerated that process. David has a congenital heart defect which means that his first weeks were spent in intensive care and high dependency units at Alder Hey Children's Hospital, and he had three open-heart surgeries before he was 5. That experience was just as hard as you imagine, and at the same time it was like a dedicated workout for my self-esteem. As difficult and triggering as so much of it was, it reminded me of my strength and pushed me out of a place of safety into a place of growth.

That theme then continued into the most important 14 months of my life, when I embarked on an affair with the man who taught me what an equal, passionate, fulfilling, romantic relationship should look like. This was not the protective safety I had looked for as a young woman. This was the intense, life-affirming, burning fire of two people truly meant to experience life together, and it brought me back to the person I was always supposed to be.

It burned bright, it burned fast, it was never meant to last very long, it ended far too soon and it hurt like nothing on this earth, but it changed both of our lives for the better and it left no scars, only strength and a renewed sense of self. It blew my life apart and it dropped me off a cliff but without it I would never have moved forward. I would never have flown.

Out of the ashes of my old life I have built my own business, my own life on my own terms, I am now telling my own story and I have a new relationship which perfectly complements my current trajectory for personal growth. I am where

I am supposed to be, I am fierce, I am free and the only person keeping me safe is me.

For some of the characters in the story of my life I am the bad guy, the problem, the cause of distress or the persistent aggravation. For others I am the inspiration, the comfort, the vital support or the hilarious company. All that matters to me is that I can support other people to own their own stories and step into the light of a life worth living. Being liked or disliked, admired or mocked, wanted or dismissed is all a part of being around other human beings.

What matters, in my experience, is being true to yourself and being fulfilled. It is my intention that this book will help you to do just that.

MARKETING YOUR BUSINESS

Time to dig into some classically 'business' issues before we wend our way back to things like self-belief, self-worth and ways we can achieve a happier life. As a business owner, marketing, networking, productivity and organisation are all absolutely crucial, so the coming chapters will focus on those elements to get you rocking along nicely from a business point of view. I have decided to begin with marketing because we cannot make very much money without it, but it is also the thing that can cause us a good deal of anxiety.

It is so easy to find businesses all over social media where their marketing strategy, if I can call it that, is to say 'I have a great product. Here it is. Buy it!' and that's it.

I understand. Marketing is scary. It's hard being out there selling your stuff. However, it is no good just sitting there saying, 'This is what I do. Buy it!' It is not going to work. Then you end up thinking, *Why aren't people buying it? Maybe it's terrible! Maybe I shouldn't be doing this!* It is not that at all; it is just that simply displaying your product to the world is not marketing.

Imagine walking into a room full of your ideal clients. This room has got loads of people in it and most of them are people who need your services or want your products. Imagine that your branding is all over the walls of that room, everywhere. Pictures of your products, your tagline is there, your logo is prominently displayed. They cannot miss it.

Also in that room are your competitors, people who do similar things to or the same thing as you, and they are talking to your ideal clients. They are going around the room chatting to people, and you are sitting in the corner, very happy about all of your branding all over the walls, but you are not talking to anybody.

Who do you think your ideal clients are going to go to?

This is a really important part of marketing – it might even be THE most important part of marketing. You cannot sell things without talking to people. Certainly not in my experience – it is not a model with which I am familiar! Social media is a particularly good example of this. People will tell you that you should be on Instagram or Facebook, or that you need a LinkedIn profile or a Twitter account. Well, that's great but just being there is not actually going to achieve anything, because you will be there as just another bit of wallpaper while people scroll.

If you are not talking to people, you are not really marketing. This is true of social media and it is true of all other kinds of marketing.

You will have heard the phrase 'people buy people'. This idea may panic you – if people buy people, does that mean you have to be the most likeable person on the planet, the person who can make friends really easily and everybody loves? Oh my goodness, if that's not you, are you feeling like you might as well pack up now? No, don't panic. That's not the case. What that phrase means is we are not really particularly logical as human beings. We go with our gut most of the time, and our emotions and instincts. What people want to know is do they like you? Are you one of them?

You do not have to be the most likeable person in the world. You will appeal to people who are like you. Everybody has a group of people where they fit in, where they belong – those are your people, and those are probably your ideal clients.

Let's be honest: when we work with people, we very rarely check out their qualifications. I don't think it's just me of whom this is true. When I chose my accountant, I didn't ask to see her certificate of qualification – I couldn't actually tell you what her qualifications are. One assumes she has them because she has a successful accountancy business! That wasn't why I chose her – I chose her because I like her and she is one of 'my people'. We get on really well, which means I can trust her; I know I can ask her anything and be honest with her. That is what is really important. I wouldn't have known those things about her if she hadn't talked to me at networking events and if we hadn't been in social media groups together where I could see her talking to and advising other people.

Those were the important things, that was how she marketed herself to me. It wasn't because her Instagram profile was full of interesting facts about accounting – which it is, but that wasn't what sold her to me.

It is really important that you actually talk, and be you. I get that that can be really scary because what if people don't like you? Yes, it feels like a huge issue, but people will like you. You have got through life this far! You will find your people. You will start off, and you will talk to a few people, and they won't get it, or you won't be their kind of person, and that's fine. You will find your people. That is really where the marketing starts to kick in.

You have to know what you offer to people. For instance, I bring calm and clarity into people's lives, so I know that my ideal clients are looking for someone who is calm and who can be clear. They are actually not bothered about whether my sense of humour is their sense of humour – it's great if we can share a joke, but it's not essential. They are not bothered about whether we would choose the same restaurants because we are probably never going to go out to dinner together. They don't have to like everything about me. You don't have to be the person they would date in order to sell something to people! You do not have to be their best friend. You have to know what you offer and you will find people for whom you are the right person for them to get that from. Not everybody will find me calming, but I can make the people who do feel so much better.

You have to find the people for whom you are the right fit.

Let's talk about the people who already know and like you. You might be worried about going out into the world and finding all of these people who are your people and who get you and who like you ... guess what? You already have a group of people in your life who know you, like you, trust you – they are your friends and family and your existing network. This might sound very obvious, but it is missed by so many people running their own businesses. Have you told all of your friends and family exactly what it is that you do, and what kind of clients you are looking for? I come across business owners who are scrabbling out there on social media for clients, trying to make relationships, but they haven't told most of their existing network that they even have a business let alone that they want some work.

Use your existing network. If I spoke to your friends, would they be able to tell me what you do and who is your ideal client? If they cannot tell me, you need to fix that. They already know you and like you, so of course they want to help you. If they come across someone who says 'I'm thinking of getting my living room done, but I don't really know what to do with it', if they know you are an interior designer, they should be saying, 'Oh my friend is really good at this, give her a call!' What a missed opportunity if they either don't really know what you do, or don't understand who would use you! They should know exactly who you are looking for.

Using your existing network is the marketing tip that so many people miss. It can be such an easy win.

You have to believe that your product or services can make someone's life better. Here is where we come to our first mindset block:

Mindset block alert!

I don't really believe in what I'm selling, which makes it hard for me to get out there and really start talking about it to friends or to strangers.

If this is all feeling very uncomfortable, take some time to dig into what you really feel about what you do. Do you really believe what you are doing can make life better for some people? Who are those people?

I hope you believe that, because it is true. That is why you started your business! Once you know that you are confident about that, you can get out there and talk to people. It is not about selling, it is not about, 'Buy this, buy this', it is just about honestly saying, 'I can help with that'.

Chasing some kind of random audience on social media is not really the way forward until you have dug into the network that you have. When I talk about your network, I don't just mean your best friends and your mum and dad, although don't be afraid to talk to them – getting a client because Aunty Gladys recommended you is brilliant, there is no shame in that! You are not a 'real' business because you get your clients from some kind of whizz bang marketing strategy. If Uncle Bob brought you four clients, that's brilliant! Thanks Uncle Bob! Buy him a bottle of whisky for Christmas. I also, though, mean your existing network just in terms of all of the people you know.

You probably have a plumber, an electrician, a car mechanic, all those kinds of people who have touched your life in some way. You have friends and acquaintances, you have people with whom you do your hobbies ... do they all know what you do? It might feel really icky to hand out flyers at your next Zumba class but you know what? People don't mind. They really don't. The worst that will happen is that they will just bin it out of their handbag when they get home; it doesn't matter, but if you haven't told them what you do, you are missing a trick. People generally want to be helpful and help others to succeed.

You have to talk about your business. I am really sorry because I know you want me to say that if you use a particular social media template, you are going to get millions more followers and make loads of sales. It doesn't work like that. You just have to be out there talking. When people say that you need to 'engage' on social media, that's just talking to people. It doesn't have to be horribly fake. If it feels horribly fake that means you are not really talking to your people – you may not have found them yet.

Get out there, find people that resonate with you, for whom you resonate, and get chatting. It doesn't have to be immediately about what you do and buying your thing – talk about their cats or whatever seems appropriate. Get talking, build those relationships. That is the best way I know to market your business.

My business has grown almost entirely through word of mouth and referrals. I have had clients come to me through social media, and, yes, that does happen more as you get a little bit bigger and more established. At the start, though, the main percentage of my work came from people recommending me and saying to their friends and contacts that they should have a chat with me.

A client said to me the other day 'I feel like I've got a real rapport with you.' She never asked me how long I've been a coach or what my qualifications were. She doesn't really care. She likes me, we get on and she feels like I 'get' her so she wants to work with me. That is really what marketing is all about.

Thinking Points

- You cannot sell things without talking to people.
- Talk, and be you. You will find your people.
- Use your existing network – they are already your people!
- It is not about selling, it is just about honestly saying, 'I can help with that.'

BE YOU, BE VISIBLE

You will have heard the phrase 'People Buy People' and it is true, but what does that mean for how you market your business?

I will tell you what it does *not* mean: it does not mean that you have to be the most likeable person in the world, so do not panic. Yes, people buy people, but it is not a popularity contest. It is about finding people who are like you; it is about being 'one of us'.

So you might think that your hobby is not 'corporate' enough or that nobody else will get why you like the TV shows you watch. Or perhaps you have obscure musical taste or an unusual fashion sense. These are things people often worry about because they imagine that revealing these things will harm their marketing. The truth is, these things *are* your marketing.

Unless you do something terribly unusual, the chances are that hundreds of people do what you do, or do something similar. So there's only so much mileage in saying, 'I do this … and I'm really good at it'. There is, however, a lot of mileage in showing up as authentically you and building relationships with like-minded people, who will then want to work with you. Guess what? No one is going to ask to see your professional qualifications. We like to think we are logical as human beings, but we are so much more emotional than we admit, and when choosing someone to work with, top of the list is 'Will I get on with this person?' It is rarely 'Are they the most qualified in their field?' – unless, perhaps, you are a heart surgeon!

Being authentically you on social media and in your other marketing avenues means that not only will you attract like-minded people but also that you will put off people with whom you really don't want to work. If someone finds your posts off-putting because your personality is shining through, that's a great way of weeding out a person you didn't want to have as a client in any case. Never worry that your authentic self will be off-putting: if someone is put off by who you are, they are not the right client for you.

We are always told we have to 'niche' and know exactly to whom we are offering our services. That doesn't have to just mean 'I coach creative people' or 'I do graphic design for sports teams'. It can also mean realising that most of your clients are into cooking, same as you are, and they have grown-up children, or they love their pets, or they are petrolheads, or into 80s music. You don't have to put that on your website, but you will gradually notice your clients tend to have the same values as you and perhaps similar life experiences – and that is a good thing. When you find 'your people', that is when the best business relationships blossom and they are far deeper relationships than those based on price or who had the shiniest website.

Yes, people buy people. But we don't all buy the *same* people. Show up authentically as yourself, don't be afraid to show who you are, and your people will find you. When they do, they will want whatever services you are offering because they will recognise that you are one of them.

Which brings us to being visible. I know, I know: showing your face on social media can be daunting. There is a whole other discussion to be had there about insecurity, standards of beauty, how we feel we 'should' look, but let's save that for another book. The truth of the matter is being visible will help you to grow your business, so you just gotta do it.

Putting up videos, doing lives, being interviewed on other people's platforms – these can all feel pretty scary. This is partly because we imagine it is similar to standing up in front of a conference – speaking on stage to a seated audience all staring up at us. Petrifying if you're not used to it!

The reality is that if you approach your video content that way, it probably won't hit the mark in any case. A better way to think about videos and lives is that they are the equivalent of chatting to a group of people in a coffee shop or in your living room. Sure, if you have a large following, there is the potential that lots of people will be watching you, but they will each be watching you by themselves. You want to make them feel as though you are chatting just to them, not giving a presentation to the multitude.

When we think of video content that way, we realise that a lot of our anxieties are unnecessary. However you would look to hang out with a group of friends, that is how you need to look to make a video. Full hair and make-up not required, this is not your slot on Oprah. This is you showing up to say 'Hi, here are my thoughts on...' whatever it is. You are sharing your thoughts, and you hope that some of the people watching will share theirs in the comments. It's a conversation, just a chat. Something friendly. Perfect lighting also not essential!

I still find going live a little nerve-wracking because if I mess up, I can't re-do it the way I can with a recorded video. But then I remember that 'messing up' isn't messing up at all. So you have to take a moment to formulate your point, or an ambulance wails past in the middle of it, or you trip over a word – that would happen in a normal conversation right? You wouldn't collapse in shame. You would just carry on or laugh or take a pause. It's just normal life; you are showing up as a normal person with thoughts to share. That's all.

Video content on social media is not the equivalent of public speaking day at school. No one is marking you. No one is going to comment on your 'performance'. No one is going to applaud you afterwards, either! It is just showing up to have your side of a conversation. Do that however is authentic to you. People buy people they can connect with. Get out there and show them who they are buying.

Thinking Points

- ♀ Show up as authentically you and build relationships with like-minded people.
- ♀ If someone is put off by who you are, they are not the right client for you.
- ♀ Show your face, show people who they are buying.

NETWORKING

Networking is just talking to people. We have discussed how important that is for marketing your business, but because it is called 'networking' rather than 'talking to people' it can sound scary and businessy and make you feel like you need to have special skills.

It is just talking to people. So calm down, you can definitely do it.

What is the point of networking? Before you get sucked in to some amazing '5-day challenge to become the world's greatest networker', what is the point of it? The point is to meet people who need your services or products or who can support you or, potentially, both. You might know a few people now who have become your clients; they were your friends or your family members, they have become your clients – that's great, but you have mined that network now. You need to meet new people. That is all networking is: going out and meeting new people who could potentially become your clients, or who could support you in your business, or both.

It is really not that complicated. Sure, there are lots of great tips out there for how to do it really effectively, but sometimes we can over complicate things. Certainly some of the bullshit I want to dispel in this book is the idea you have to have read a guide or learned a process in order to do things that are really fairly basic. Telling people what you do and how you can help them, going out and talking to people, that is marketing and networking. You don't need it to be a huge thing in your head where you have to learn loads of techniques. If you are really interested and you want to learn lots of new techniques and dig into these things, go for it, but I don't want you to be held back in your business because you feel like you can't go to a networking event because you haven't yet learned 'how to network'.

You have been networking your whole life. You have gone to the pub. I'm sure you have gone out and met the friends of your friend. You have gone on a night out and met some new people. That's networking. It's just at that point you might not have had anything to sell, so you didn't realise it was networking. It is, and that is all it is.

If you have found yourself in the past at some kind of networking event that made you feel really uncomfortable and totally out of your depth, you didn't know what you were doing and you felt stupid and you never want to go there again, thank you, Helen ... that is because you were at the wrong networking event. It is not because you are terrible at networking. If you are in a room full of people who make you feel uncomfortable, who intimidate you or who don't make you feel welcome, that is not your fault. It might not be their fault either; it might just be that they are not your people, and that's not with whom you should be networking.

I will share with you my experience of networking as an employee and then my experience of networking as a business owner, because they are very different. I used to work in the marketing team of a law firm in Manchester, and I helped to run a few networking events, and I attended a few. Often, I would attend the sort of events where there is a speaker and you are going to learn something interesting, so it is really worthwhile, even if the networking over coffee is a bit intimidating. These kinds of events were what I thought networking was, and it did feel intimidating, and I did feel out of my depth. Because, at the time, I didn't really have anything particular to sell, I didn't really know what it was I needed from these people, and they were not really my kind of people. It was all a bit pointless.

When I started my own business I knew I needed to get out there and do some networking. I thought, *Okay, I'm a bit older now; I am sure I can put on my big girl pants and manage this networking stuff.* So I went along to a local women in business networking event, and I cannot tell you how different it was. This was a room full of people like me. They were mainly middle-aged women, mostly mothers but not entirely, who ran their own businesses and who were all from my local area. We had such a great time. We just chatted. We exchanged business cards and told each other what we did, but we just had a good natter and a bit of giggle, and I met people who have now become clients, suppliers and really good friends.

That is what good networking looks like. So if it is not feeling like that, you are probably not in the right networking group.

I said that the point of networking is to meet people who need your services or who can support you, or both. I would say that far more important than networking with your ideal clients is networking with people who can support you, who you find supportive, and who you can support. It's about finding your business 'gang'. Some of them are bound to turn out to be your ideal clients, but even if they don't, if you get a group of people together who all support each other in their businesses and who all turn to each other when they have a problem, who chat through issues and challenges, that group is going to refer business to each other.

Some networking groups have strict rules about referrals, and you have to refer this many people to other members of the group ... the thing is, it should happen naturally. If you are in my business gang, even if I know that I am never going to use your services and you are probably never going to use mine, if I like you and we get on and we support each other, I am going to be referring you all over the place.

It is more important to find a group where you feel really comfortable and where you can support each other, and then the referrals will come even if the people in that group specifically are not necessarily your ideal clients. That is much better than to be in a room full of people who potentially need your services but with whom you don't really get on, with whom you don't really gel. You are not going to make many sales that way.

There are different kinds of networking events – there are ones you have to pay for and there are free ones. I have paid a few quid to attend a particular event, but I have never signed up to one of these big paid-for networking groups. As yet. I haven't felt like I have needed to because there are some amazing free and low-cost groups to attend. I would say paying for networking when you are just starting out is quite a big outlay that you might not get much back from, so I would recommend looking into the free and low-cost options first.

It is important to find ones at which you are comfortable, and it is important to go semi-regularly. People will tell you that you have to be there at every event, but that's not necessarily the case. Our lives are busy – you do not have to commit to being there every week, but if you are a fairly familiar face within that group, it will be good for your business. You are going to have to attend a few where you only attend once, just to see if it is the group for you, but once you find ones that you like, try to attend as much as you can.

The great thing is that a lot of these networking groups also have social media groups and online platforms, so you can continue to network online.

Another important point is following up after networking events. Some people are really good at following up and it not sounding fake, but I find it really difficult. If I have met you at a networking event, I am probably going to find you on LinkedIn and connect with you and have a look at your posts. If I think there is a post upon which I can comment, I will do so, but I am not going to be sending you a fake private message, it's just not me. Follow up, but find a real reason to do so. Say something real, even if it's just 'We were both at that event; wasn't the speaker a bit weird?' Be real with people.

Following up doesn't have to be 'Do you remember me?

Here are my services – buy them!' In fact, please don't do that. If you have met people at an event whom you liked or who you felt could be an ideal client, follow up in some way, even if it is just connecting with them on social media and making a note to yourself to check in with them now and again to see if you can comment on their posts and start building that relationship.

It really does take time. You might go to a networking event, meet somebody who needs your services, and they call you the next day, and you've got a client. It could happen. I wouldn't go with the attitude that that is what you need to get out of it though, because sometimes these things can be a really slow burn. When I look back to when I first met that brilliant group of women, it was over two years ago at time of writing. At this point, most of them are clients of mine or I am a client of theirs, or both. That didn't happen the day after the networking event though, it has taken time. Obviously, looking back, it was time well spent, but at the time I didn't know that; I didn't know it was going to come to anything. I just knew that I liked these people, and I wanted to chat with them more and go to more events where they were.

It can take time, but it is worth it. You will slowly expand your network. You will see people online who seem really well connected, who are always commenting and seem to know everyone; they have inside jokes with everybody and they make you feel like you don't belong and don't know what you are doing ... That is because they have taken the time. They were not like that when they started. They have taken the time, built up their network and they are now comfortable with it.

You will end up feeling that comfortable with a large proportion of your network, over time.

The best thing you can do, if you want to build relationships within a network, is to be supportive. There is that Maya Angelou quote about people not remembering what you said or did but they will remember how you made them feel. It is so true. If you are the one celebrating other people's wins, wishing them happy birthday, saying nice things about photos of their children ... what people will start to think is you are a lovely person. That is great. It means they probably want to work with you, and all that has to happen then is they need to get to a point where they need your services, and then you will make a sale.

Be supportive to your network and they will be supportive to you, which is invaluable when you are running a business. It is a lonely old thing to be doing, so finding and having a supportive network is a win in itself, but it can also lead to business for sure. Be generous. Introduce people to each other. If you meet someone that you really like but you can't really do much for each other, you might know a person who is their ideal client, so make an introduction. If you are generous in that way, it will benefit everybody, including you.

Networking is not that scary or difficult. It is just talking to people, and it takes time. Find people with whom you are comfortable. If you are feeling uncomfortable, you are not terrible at networking, you are just in the wrong group. Go and find the right group for you.

Thinking Points

- Networking is talking to people.
- Networking is going out and meeting new people who could potentially become your clients, or who could support you in your business, or both.
- You have been networking your whole life, you just did not realise it.
- If it is not feeling comfortable, you are probably not in the right networking group.
- Follow up after networking events, and be supportive of your network.
- Seeing these relationships come to fruition takes time, but it is worth it.

PRODUCTIVITY

If we have marketed ourselves effectively and are doing a great job with our networking, chances are our sales will be coming in and we are gaining new clients. So we have a lot of work to do! This is the time that business owners start to worry about their productivity and ask themselves why they cannot do as much in a day or in a week as they would like to. The answer to that is: you cannot get out what you do not put in.

Productivity is your output: what you get done, what you produce, what you create, what you do in your day. Your output. I say output because we are going to be remembering that we are all basically machines. I mean that we need to remember that we have output, and we also have input, and we also need maintenance. Without remembering these things, the output is going to be a problem.

You can't work properly without proper care. You wouldn't expect your car to keep running continually without an MOT or a service or an oil change or, at the very least, some fuel. You would know that your car was going to break down, stop working for you, start showing warning lights, something would fall off – you know that's going to happen if you don't take care of your car. The same goes for all the appliances in your house. You get your boiler regularly serviced, you keep an eye on your appliances, you know that after a certain amount of time, if they don't have any maintenance, they're probably going to need to be replaced … we know this. This is how machinery works.

We forget it when it applies to us.

Your output is dependent upon your input and the maintenance you do for yourself.

You may have thought this chapter would be my five tips for being hugely productive. In fact, I will be talking about the maintenance and the input. Without those, we cannot create more or better productivity. It just can't be done. We're not going to be able to do all the things we want to do or improve our processes if we don't look at the input and the maintenance.

What is your manual? If you were a machine, what would it say in your operating manual? I'll tell you what it says in mine. The Helen Machine needs:

* a good night's sleep, pretty much every night
* coffee – two cups a day
* fresh air
* reasonably healthy food
* sunshine & water – just like a houseplant.

Then there are the things that are a bit more unique to me. What is in your manual that is only about you? Is there a particular form of exercise that you know is going to make you feel so much better? Do you need time by yourself, peace and quiet and a bit of headspace? Do you need to be around people? Do you get stressed when you don't see people enough? Do you need contact? What kind of rest do you need: a full night's sleep every night, a good lie-in at the weekends, a cat nap in the day? Do you need regular sex? It doesn't have to be sex with anybody else – do you need regular sex with yourself? That is one of our needs, and if that need isn't being met, we are a stress ball of irritability and a general pain in the arse to be around.

These are the things that need to be in the operating manual that we keep in our heads or that we write down somewhere. If thinking about what you actually need is new to you, write it down. I have a list of my needs written down, some that are basic and some that are unique to me, and I need those things to happen or for those needs to be met or for me to do those things if I am going to perform at my best.

What is your manual and what do you personally need?

Then it's about understanding your processes. It is not just about what puts you in the best position to perform, it is also about when can you perform at your best? What are your personal processes? Are you a morning person? Do you work best in the evenings? If you have something really hard to do, is it best to do it in private, in peace, or do you find it best to do really hard things when you have somebody with you?

It is really important that you understand your personal processes and then work with them. Rather than booking meetings for the mornings if you know that's your most productive time, make sure that's the time you set aside to do the really hard stuff. Then have the meetings at three o'clock in the afternoon when you're in a bit of a slump, because we don't need to be at our best for just talking to people. Or maybe that's not true for you: maybe you are an introvert and talking to people is the hardest part of your day, in which case you do need to schedule that for the time when you are at your optimum.

Let's take a moment to talk about forgiving ourselves. We all have these needs, unique needs; we all have our own operating manual and our own processes. So often, we get tangled up because we then feel bad about the realities. If you are a person who doesn't really get going until eleven o'clock in the morning, there is no point spending your life feeling guilty for not being one of those up-at-seven-and-out-the-door kind of people. Just forgive yourself! You are you. It's fine. It's totally acceptable.

Rather than spendings days thinking, *I must be better at this, I must get up earlier, I must be better in the mornings* ... you just need to set up your day so that you can be productive at a time that works for you. The biggest barrier to having a productive day and a working pattern that really works for us is our guilt and our self-loathing and the stories we tell ourselves about what we should be able to do. Forgive yourself for being you.

Don't expect your machine to work without maintenance. Look after yourself and prioritise yourself.

Plan a break. I say that because a lot of us don't just need maintenance. Especially if all of this is a little bit new to you, your machine might well need to be switched off, completely stripped down, overhauled and restarted. Do you need a break? Hint: the answer is yes you do, because we all do. So plan one, and again, forgive yourself for needing one.

Mindset Block Alert!

I cannot possibly take a long break and go away somewhere by myself.

Yes, you can, but you cannot do it without prioritising yourself, asking for help, imposing on the people around you and using the community you have. That is how we function together as a community – we impose upon people. How sad would it be if we never needed each other? If nobody ever needed you and you never needed anyone, it would be really sad. If the way to get you a break is to ask for help and impose on the people around you, that's what you've got to do.

I told you this wasn't going to be easy stuff! The good news is, though, that you can then repay it. Let's say that you have a partner or a spouse and you say 'Oh good grief, I really need a weekend just by myself. You are going to have to look after the kids the whole weekend. I get that that's going to be really challenging, but I just need it. I tell you what, though, darling, we will also plan the same for you! In another few weeks you can have a whole weekend off!' So it's fair and everybody gets the reset time they need.

What does that have to do with productivity? Your machine might need more than just maintenance. If you are tired and stressed all the time, and things feel like a really huge effort all the time, you need to accept that you are extremely tired and you have been for ages, which is why it feels normal. It is time to take a break and reset. There is nothing I can tell you, there is no magic formula for making an exhausted person productive. You have got to stop and take a reset. You are not lazy. You are not crap. Stop with those stories. You do, however, need to take responsibility for your machine.

It turns out that the answer to being more productive is to look after yourself. You will be amazed at what you can achieve and how much more you can get done when you are actually looking after your machine.

Thinking Points

- ♡ Productivity is your output.
- ♡ Your output is dependent upon your input and the maintenance you do for yourself.
- ♡ What is your operating manual?
- ♡ How can you get creative and involve your community to ensure your needs are met?
- ♡ Take responsibility for maintaining your machine.

FINDING FOCUS, BEING COMFORTABLE, DOING LESS

One of the hardest things to find sometimes is focus. Motivation. As an extension of my thoughts on productivity, let me share with you my favourite tip for finding some focus when all you want to do is hide under the duvet.

Use a timer

The first part of using the timer is to choose a timescale that feels safe for you. On a really bad day, that safe timescale might easily be just 5 minutes. It often is for me. You feel as though you can just about manage to do 5 minutes of something before you flop back down on the couch. Okay. 5 minutes *it is*. Or 10, 15, 30 – *whatever feels like the right timescale for how you are feeling*. Self-forgiveness is key.

Once you have your timescale, choose your task. What needs your focus today? Don't panic – it's only going to be 5 minutes. So you can pick one of those big, horrible, head-space-filling jobs because it's only going to be your safe timescale that you use for this. No one is asking you to sit down for hours and finish something.

Got your timescale? Got your task?

Set a timer, probably on your phone, and go for it. Spend your chosen amount of time working on that task. When the timer goes off, you are done. Give yourself a pat on the back. You focused on that task for your chosen amount of time. You did it!

What will that achieve? In my experience a number of things:

* You will have made a start. That mental block about doing *anything* has been pushed away.
* You will have made progress on your chosen task. You will be amazed by what you can achieve, even in just 5 minutes.
* You might find you feel motivated to do a little more now that you have done the hard part and got started. (You might not, and that's okay too.)
* You will know how much you can achieve in your chosen timescale. Your tasks won't seem so over-whelming when you realise they don't take up as much time as you imagine.

You can set the timer and focus on a task any time of the day when you feel able to do so. Asking for open-ended focus and motivation from yourself is probably unrealistic at the moment. What timescale feels right for you today? Go with that. It will be different tomorrow.

Great tip right? Maybe so, or maybe it is not for you. When

it comes to productivity you will find an endless supply of hints and tips online. Many of which are very valuable. The most important question, though, is: what works for you?

If you run your own business, you have the freedom to work in a way that makes you the most productive. All you have to do is take away any value judgements you ascribe to certain things.

What do I mean by that?

You may have heard that superproductive people get up early and work for two hours before their kids are awake. Maybe some people do, and good luck to them. They have found what works for them. But if you are a night owl, or if your most creative time is after lunch, getting up at 5 a.m. is not going to magically make you productive. It is going to make you tired and grumpy.

There is nothing wrong with working in your PJs. There is nothing wrong with only being productive in the afternoons. There is nothing wrong with writing social media posts whilst out for a walk. All that matters is what helps you to get the job done.

Before you start the next and latest fad for productivity, ask yourself these questions:

* When am I at my most creative?
* When do I feel the least motivated?
* Where do I feel the most comfortable?
* Which working environment makes me feel the most happy?

If the answer to the third question is 'in bed', well, that is where I have done a significant amount of writing, so I practise what I preach! I am sometimes far more productive sitting under the duvet than I would be at my office desk.

Once you have the answer to those questions, that should give you some indications of where and when you need to be working in order to get the most done.

Of course, there are constraints on that, but at least you can now see your optimum. The next step is getting creative so you can achieve that optimum as often as possible, whatever the constraints may be.

The person who will benefit from you being at your most productive is you. You are not answerable to anyone who tells you to 'just work in the evenings' or 'go for a morning run'. If those things work for you, great! If they don't, you are not a productivity failure, you just need a different plan.

Write the [your name here] Plan for Productivity. That is the only plan that matters.

You might be thinking, *That's wonderful, Helen, but I have loads of ideas and never seem to get anything done. I always have loads of projects on the go at once, I work really hard, I am always busy, but nothing ever seems to get completed. Timers and sofas are not going to cut it.*

I have worked on this situation with a number of clients and the way forward is often to do less. Or rather, to do everything but in order, rather than trying to do all of the things all of the time.

Whenever we have a new idea, it feels like the most exciting thing, the most important thing and the thing that needs to be done now. Yet if we give in to that feeling every time, we end up with lots of half-finished ideas on the go and no time to get anything completed. It is loads of fun to start something new, but if you truly want to make progress, you need to work through projects one at a time.

So how to begin? Make a list of all of the projects you have on the go, the ideas you have, the things you are trying to get done. If any of them no longer feel like the right thing to be doing, cross them off. There is no need to finish anything just for the sake of it – if something isn't working, it can be binned.

Do any of these projects go in an obvious order? For instance, are you trying to launch something new and also sort out your social media platforms? The platforms probably need to come first so you have a way of promoting your new product. Go through the list and put the projects in order of when they need to get done, when you would like them to get done, and how they make sense in terms of the coming weeks and months.

Next, allocate one project to each month. Project one will get done next month, project two the month after and so on. Yes, I know that means your list probably runs years into the future. That is okay – we are now dealing with reality instead of fantasy.

What does this plan achieve? Firstly, it gives you a focus for each month. There will be no more procrastination because you will know what you should be doing, how you should be spending any bits of time that you have, what the priorities are.

Secondly, it means that things will actually start to get

done. Will you have everything done in a couple of months? No, but you never would have done anyway. What you will have done in a couple of months is two projects. In a year you will have done twelve. You may even do more, because if you complete one project in a couple of weeks there is nothing to stop you from starting the next one. The time-scales may change, but one thing is certain: completion will actually happen.

Thinking Points

- ♀ Use a timer when focus feels hard.
- ♀ Figure out *your* plan for productivity.
- ♀ Order your projects and complete one at a time.

ORGANISATION

This is a topic that I have always been well known for – if you ask anybody to sum me up in one word, they are likely to say organised. I am going to share a few of my tips here with you and also some thought processes around who you are and the fact that there is no point trying to replicate me in you. This is a guide to being organised, whoever you are.

Tip number one:

Write everything down. I really mean everything, especially if you are stressed out. The more stressed out I get, the more basic things I have to write down. My kids get bathed and showered probably a couple of times a week – if that doesn't seem enough, don't judge me! – but I absolutely have it on my to-do list. If I get to Thursday, and I'm thinking they need a bath tonight, that goes on the to-do list. I am not going to even try to remember anything without writing it down.

The reason being, I have realised, yes, I feel like I can't trust my memory, but more than that, I don't actually want to trust my memory. My memory is great for song lyrics ... song lyrics and things that I did years ago that were embarrassing; that's the kind of stuff I remember, that is basically what my memory is good for. I use a huge number of my mental processes to be productive, to get the stuff done I want to get done. I do not want to waste any of my mental bandwidth on remembering stuff, so it all gets written down.

I am not at my desk all the time, but the one thing I have with me all the time is, of course, my phone. If you are as welded to your phone as I am to mine, you will know it is a great place to keep notes and reminders. It doesn't actually matter where you keep these things because we will come on in a moment to how you gather these things all together. It is best to have only a few places where you keep things, but I wouldn't say just one, though. I have an online calendar, I have a project management system that my team and I use, and I have in the past used a notepad app on my phone. Maybe two or three places maximum for you to keep things, but write it all down: when you have a thought, when there is something you want to remember, write it down somewhere.

What do we do with all that stuff? We don't want to be looking at all of those notes every day because that would be overwhelming. As soon as we feel overwhelmed we can't do anything – it doesn't matter how organised we are, we are not going to get anything done.

Tip number two:

Each morning, gather your list for the day. I sit down with my coffee first thing in the morning – I haven't even got out of bed – I'm still in my PJs, and I get my notebook, as I personally like a pen and paper for the daily list. I look in all the places where I keep my information, most things have due dates attached, so I pull together my list for the day. That is just that day. Every other day can just wait – I don't have to worry about what's happening tomorrow because it's all written down somewhere; I am concentrating on today and what is on my list for today.

A really important part of being organised is keeping yourself sane. If you are feeling stressed and overwhelmed, it's all too much and your head is full, it is very difficult to get anything done. That's when people might say 'You are so scatty' or 'You are so all over the place'. You might not be, you might be very organised, but you are just trying to organise too many things, all inside your head, all at once. Let's try to reduce some of that noise. With that in mind...

Tip number three:

Pick three things at a time. Your brain can cope much better if it has a list of three things in front of it than a list of twenty things. It's just how it is, it's just how we work. You have your list for the day, it could have all kinds of things on it, it could be huge, it could be small ... pick the three things that you are going to work on next. That is the list in front of you. Straightaway you feel way calmer because there are only three things.

When you've done those things, you pick the next three things. It's all got to get done, but just focus on three things at a time.

A lot of organisation is just staying calm so that you can keep moving and keep doing. Then it all gets done and you feel organised.

If organisation really doesn't come naturally to you, it is just not your skill set, you know it's not you, you have tried … just admit that and forgive yourself. I know so many incredible, creative people who come to me for administrative support from my team, and they are almost apologetic for being chaotic and disorganised. My thought is that they don't need to apologise for that! They are creative people, they are creating incredible things that I wouldn't even have the first clue how to create, and they are putting them out there into the world and making it a better place with their products and services. They don't need to apologise for not also being able to do my job!

We are all hugely impressed by organised people, but it is not the be-all and end-all. Just forgive yourself if it is not you, and then find an organised person to work with. A VA, a friend, a family member, somebody to whom it comes naturally to be organised. Ask for their help. It doesn't matter that you are not organised – there is no point going through the rest of your life saying, 'I wish I could be more organised, I need to get organised …' Why not just ask somebody to help you with it if it is really not your forte?

Having said that, you actually might be a very organised person, even though right now you are saying that you are all over the place and scatty and forgetful. That might not be anything to do with your natural skill set. That might be because you are trying to do way too much or you are trying to do it in a way that doesn't work for you. In the last chapter we looked at working with your natural processes and your natural rhythms. We all have a way we work that is us, and times of the day we are at our best, and times of the month when we are at our best. Particularly women: we have a monthly rhythm. We have a week of being hugely productive and creative and full of ideas, then we have a couple of normal weeks, then we have a week where everything is hard and we can't really be bothered. That is our natural rhythm and we have to learn to work with those things, rather than trying to shoehorn ourselves into what somebody else has told us is the ideal routine or the ideal working day. Bin all of that.

Asking for help is definitely one of the top tips for a happier life.

Thinking Points

- ♀ Write everything down.
- ♀ Start each day by gathering your list.
- ♀ Have only three things on the list that is in front of you at any one time.
- ♀ Ask for help.

HOW DO I FIND THE TIME?

This is a question I get asked on a regular basis, and it is a question I have helped some of my coaching clients to answer. There are numerous time management strategies, but for women running their own businesses I have found the following to be really helpful, including for me.

The solution? A four-weekly rolling schedule.

Don't panic! It's not that complicated. The idea behind it is when we try to fit everything into every week we, inevitably, don't have the time. If we are running our own businesses, we have to do the actual work for our clients, come up with content for our social media platforms, find time to develop our businesses and also network to build new relationships. There is no way that can all be fitted into a standard week!

However, in reality it does not need to be. Having a focus for the time we have available can make it much easier to get stuff done, rather than trying to do everything piecemeal all the time.

So, for example, I now have a four-week schedule which looks like this:

Week 1 – focus on client work
Week 2 – focus on networking
Week 3 – focus on content creation
Week 4 – focus on business development.

Does this mean that I only work for clients one week out of every month? No, of course not. What it means is that in Week 1, almost everything I am doing is client work, so that week I can get done any work that I need to do for clients which is monthly. I can get ahead as much as possible to free up time over the next three weeks.

Then in Weeks 2, 3 and 4, I make sure that I set aside time for that week's focus. It also means that I know what to say no to. If it is content creation week, I don't want to be filling my time with meetings – I'm trying to write a social media schedule, email newsletters, blog posts and so on. I need decent blocks of time in which to do that. In my networking week, though, that's when I want to be booking in lots of coffees and catch-ups.

It's all about the focus.

A coaching client of mine has been trying out a similar structure. She only has one day per week when she doesn't see clients, and she was trying to use that day for everything, every week. We have tweaked this, though, so that now in Week 1 that day is for admin, in Week 2 it's for content creation, in Week 3 it's for networking and in Week 4 it's for business development. That way she can focus on getting all of one thing done for the month in one day, without trying to fit in everything every time.

There is no one time management system that works for everybody, so if this sounds like a nightmare to you, you're not 'wrong' not to use it. If it sounds like it could be the answer, though, why not give it a go?

SELF-BELIEF

We have talked about mindset blocks ... this chapter is pretty much all mindset blocks. I am talking about why it feels so hard to put into practice all of the things that we have talked about so far.

We have talked about marketing your business, networking, being productive, getting organised. Why is it so hard to put these things into practice?

I will tell you what the answer is not. The answer is not that you are lazy, that you are useless, rubbish, whatever other wonderful self-talk you have been giving yourself. That is not the reason why, so you can put all of that aside right now.

There are two reasons why it is hard to put into practice all of the useful hints and tips you read and come across in life. Those reasons are: feeling overwhelmed and a lack of self-belief.

Let's start with overwhelm. We all experience that; it is totally understandable, and most of the time it is down to the fact that we have so much going on in our lives. We are all extremely busy, and feeling overwhelmed is almost inevitable with the amount of stuff we try to pack in. The key thing is if there are things that you really do want to try or to put into practice, do not think about it as one big job. We are talking about pretty big stuff here: organisation, mindset, sorting your shit out. This is big stuff, and it is not stuff that you can do in an afternoon, even if you did have a whole afternoon to spare.

If you write down 'Marketing' on a to-do list, you are never going to get to that. You are going to look at that and think, *Eek that looks huge, I am overwhelmed by that, I cannot possibly touch it.* The way to do it is to break it down into next steps. Even then, though, when we talk about next steps, I think that sometimes we do not break things down enough. You could say to yourself the next steps for sorting out your marketing are writing a social media strategy and talking to someone who knows about Google adverts and figuring out your branding ... so you write down Social Media Strategy, Branding, Adverts as three separate tasks but, again, you are going to look at those and think they are massive jobs, and you would be right. Not necessarily as massive as you think it is, but this is chunky stuff.

When I say break it down into the next steps, I genuinely mean the very next thing you need to do. So, for instance, it could be that you need to find someone to run your Facebook adverts for you, but even that is not the very next step. Unless you already have someone in mind, in which case the next step is to email them or call them, the very next step could be to ask in a networking group if anyone knows someone who can help you with social media advertising. Or to ask your friend who advertises on social media who they use to help them. That is the very next step. Send the email; ask that question.

If you are like me and you need a new notebook for everything, then yes buying the notebook is a legitimate next step as long as it is not the only step you take! You have to actually put something into the notebook as well. Really try, though, to break down your projects into the very next step, and, crucially, you do not need to know all of the steps before you do the first one.

Just get the first one and do it.

After that, do the next one.

You will know what the very next thing you have to do is. That's the easy bit, the first step on a path even if you can't see the whole journey; the first step is obvious because it's the one right in front of you. Do that, and then do the next thing, and those are the things you want to put on the to-do list, to stop you from feeling overwhelmed by that big project.

Now let's talk about lack of self-belief. This is another really key area, and sometimes we mask this by saying, 'I haven't got time' or 'I'm overwhelmed', but deep down it's the feeling that you can't really do it.

Mindset Block Alert!

As ambitious as I am, deep down I don't really believe that I belong in this space, that I can really pull this off.

If that mindset block resonates with you, write it down. Your self-belief is not where it needs to be. It is okay to look that full in the face. If you write down, 'I don't really believe I can do this', does not mean you have to pack up and close the business. That mindset block is a mindset, it is not the truth. It is not real. You don't believe you can do it, but you can. What it means, though, is that you need to look at that lack of self-belief and do something about it. It needs some work.

Not having self-belief is often talked about as Imposter Syndrome. It's the feeling that at any moment somebody is going to find out what a big fraud you are. Any moment now, and you are tense, you are ready for it, you are going to get that email or phone call or comment that shows that someone has seen through you. They know you don't know what you are doing; they know you are winging it and you don't have the qualifications or the depth of knowledge. They are going to point that out and you are going to shrivel up and die, and it will be all over.

It is a horrible feeling. The fact that we all go through it doesn't really help, because in our minds we can think, *Yeah, everyone goes through it, but it's not real for them. But for me it IS real. I really AM a big fraud!* It is crazy, we all have that feeling. We are all winging it to an extent. What you think may be true, but the bit you are missing out is the fact that it doesn't matter. No, you may not know absolutely everything about your area of expertise. Perhaps Stephen Hawking could be said to be someone who knew everything about his area of expertise, but there are so few people in this world where you can say yep, they know absolutely everything about their thing. That is not normal!

It is not only the people who are the best at what they

do who deserve to be in the arena. Imagine if that was true. Imagine if the only people who could do ballet were prima ballerinas. Top-of-the-line dancers, the Nureyevs of this world. They are the only people who can ever do ballet. You can't do it for a hobby, your kids can't do it, nope only the people who are the best. For a start, how would anyone ever become the best? But also, it would be pretty boring.

You can apply that to anything. Imagine if top chefs were the only people who were allowed to cook. Formula 1 racers were the only people who were allowed to drive.

You can see what I'm saying. The arena is huge, for anything you want to try or anything you already have some skills at. Yes, there are people at one end of it who are the exceptional people, the absolute top. Serena Williams in tennis, and here we all are at the other end having a tennis game on a Saturday. You are still allowed to play tennis, though. Nobody is going to come up and tell you that they have realised you are not a Williams sister so what the hell are you doing on the court?

Yet in business we imagine that is just what will happen. We imagine someone will turn around and say 'Wait a minute! You are not Bill Gates! Why the hell are you managing my IT? Who do you think you are?' It will not happen, for many reasons, but partly because not everybody can afford Bill Gates, even if he did do consultancy! There are a huge number of people, though, who need IT services. So who is going to provide that for them? If you are sitting in a corner rocking because you are not the best, who is going to help them with their IT? They need someone they can afford to help them out with some stuff that you know about, so you had probably better uncurl yourself and go do the job.

You have skills and passions that can help people. That is why you started in business – that is the whole point. There are things you can do that other people need. Sometimes other people need your skills because they cannot do those things themselves, and sometimes it is because they do not have the time to do those things themselves. They need you, and it doesn't matter that you are not the most qualified or you do not have the greatest depth of knowledge. As long as you are acting in good faith, not trying to hoodwink anyone or lie about your abilities, you absolutely deserve to be in the arena.

Here's the real thing, no bullshit: there is no magic formula for finding self-belief. I am really sorry to say that, but the truth is building self-belief is like building muscle. You have got to make yourself ache and feel uncomfortable to build up to the next level. You have to actually just do the stuff. You don't want to injure yourself and push yourself too far too fast, you don't want to completely destroy yourself. You just need to push yourself that little bit further each time.

All of these things you want to do, just do a little bit of them. Then a little bit more. It is exactly like building muscle, you need to work on your self-belief muscles. It will hurt, just a bit. If it doesn't ache a bit, you are not pushing far enough. Just a little bit of discomfort, and then suddenly you will realise what was hard at the beginning is a piece of cake now! You can lift those weights, you can do that networking event, you won't remember why you ever found it hard. It comes from practice and your belief that you can do these things will be there, and then it will be on to the next challenge. The stuff you thought you could never possibly do is now the next step!

It is a little bit circular. You cannot do the stuff because you don't have the self-belief, and you don't have the self-belief because you haven't done the stuff. You have to get on that wheel, just make that first next step. Whatever is that tiny next step, do that. Then figure out what is the next step. Pretty soon you will look back and see how far you have come.

Thinking Points

- ♀ Break down projects and tasks into the very next tiny steps, and do one step after another.
- ♀ You do not need to be able to see all the steps in order to make a start: you only need to be able to see the next step.
- ♀ You deserve to use your skills and passions to help people and to make a living.
- ♀ Building your self-belief muscles takes time and practice. There is no magic formula.

SELF-WORTH

We're getting into the real stuff now folks! I truly believe that self-worth is the key to absolutely everything.

All the stuff you have read and taken in about how to get to where you want to be ... you have those dreams, you have those goals, but do you really truly deep-down believe you are worth your own time, care and investment?

Mindset Block Alert!

Deep down I don't really believe I am worth my own time, care and investment.

A lot of people do not have self-worth and a lot of us have been through the stage of not having it. You do not have to fix it right now, but if your self-worth needs some work, let's look that full in the face and recognise it is something which needs to be tackled.

Without that sense of self-worth, it is really hard to get stuff done. We are not talking about easy things here: we are talking about building a business; we are talking about getting the most out of life. Without the sense you are worth investment, you are worth the time spent on these things, you are not going to get there. If you do not really believe you are worth it, once things are hard or you have to stand up for yourself or you need to prioritise yourself, it is not going to happen.

If you have the sense you are worth time, care and investment, it is such a game changer.

Let's look at why you may not have it and why some of us have not had it in the past. It is big stuff as I say: we are looking at the deep-rooted old crap we have all carried with us from the 'wonder' that is childhood. We have all got a big bag of crap, it is just part of life, and those of us who are parents, our kids are going to have a big bag of crap too. We try not to make that bag too big for them, but they are going to have it and they are going to have to dig into it themselves. That big ol' bag we are carrying around from our formative years is one of the things we have to open up and delve into to find our sense of self-worth.

Sadly, the other reason that self-worth is hard to come by is that quite often we have someone in our lives or people in our lives who are actively working against our self-worth. They are actively working against our sense that we are worth anything. Yes, at the extreme end of this we have abusive relationships, and it is not always easy to spot if you are in one of those, but even if you are not, there might be people who just subtly, without even meaning to, undermine your sense of self-worth because of their own stuff. Drip drip, every day.

It is something else to note down, look at and realise it needs to be dealt with in some way.

We are not going to solve this in one chapter. It is not going to be the 1–4 steps to gain self-worth, but if you write these things down, you can decide if and how you are going to work on them. Knowing these are issues is the first, really important step.

Here's the thing. This is the absolute truth. Are you ready?

No matter who you are, no matter what you have done (we have all done stuff, nobody is perfect), no matter what you have been through, you are not worth less or more than any other human being.

Read that again.

There is no scale on which you are being measured. I know, I know you feel like there is. There is some massive scale, hanging in the sky, that everyone is measured against and you are not measuring up. No. There is no scale. There are no points to be obtained. There is no first place, there is no last place. You have the same worth as everybody else.

To yourself, in your own life, you need to be the most valuable person in the world.

I am guessing that you are now thinking, *Hang on, I've got kids, I've got a spouse, I've got a family, I have people who are hugely valuable to me, I cannot be the most valuable person in my world!* If that is your thought, you are imagining what I am saying is you have to put yourself first every time. No, of course not. There are, of course, going to be times when we all rightly choose to prioritise the needs of the people we love. That is a day-to-day calculation we don't even think about: who needs what, who needs the most, who needs this right now, who is the most important in this situation? Discovering your self-worth does not mean insisting what *you* need is always the most important thing!

However, bear this in mind: there is no one else, nobody else on this whole planet, with whom you will spend every single second of your life, other than you. No one. There is no one else who is in control of your inner self-talk. Just you. There is nobody else who is in control of how you treat your body and of the choices you make to keep yourself safe and make your life beautiful. Nobody else. Just you. There is only you.

If you do not place the most value on yourself, as everybody else should place the most value on themselves, where are you left? You are lost, as many of us are and have been, without a foundation. As Dr Brené Brown would say, you are left 'hustling for your worthiness' because you are not giving it to yourself. You are the only person to whom you should be the most valuable, all the time. It is your life.

It is sad because most of us spend our whole lives trying to find that person or that achievement, that status or the thing we can buy that is going to make us feel as though we have worth. We keep running down that tunnel towards a mythical prize, and you know what? We have no need to run. All any of us needs to do is just stop, reach down and pick up our self-worth. It is ours for the taking; it is right there. We just pick it up and give it to ourselves. We do not need to be running, running, trying to find that thing, that person, that next relationship, if we buy this, if we achieve that, then we are going to have worth … just pick it up. Nobody is going to give it to you. Just pick it up. Look down, it is right there. Pick it up. It's yours.

Believe me, I remember not having it. I remember chasing the things I thought would give it to me, and how, at that point, I really did not understand what people were saying to me when they told me that it was just inside me. So if what I am saying sounds like *Alice Through The Looking Glass* shit, I understand. As much as the answer is simple, that does not mean it is easy.

If you need support to dig into this, I highly recommend that you speak to a coach or a counsellor or a therapist. Any kind of coaching or talking therapy will, at some point, touch on your self-worth because it is so crucial to what you want to achieve. Coaching and therapy are not just things you seek out when you are in crisis. Why would you wait until that point before you look into the support you can have? This is about getting you to the place where you need to be; it is about digging through the crap that is holding you back. Now is the time to do that. Anybody in mental health or personal development will say: Please come to us sooner rather than later, do not wait until you are in crisis. Let's get this stuff under control now.

Your mental health and your future happiness are worthy of investment. If you invest in the upkeep of your household appliances, why would you not invest in your own health and happiness? You are worth more than the material things around you.

I truly believe that having self-worth is the crucial answer to getting everything you need and want. Getting some help with that is probably the best investment you will ever make.

Thinking Points

- 💡 Self-worth is the key to everything.
- 💡 You are not worth less or more than any other human being.
- 💡 There is no scale on which you are being measured. There are no points to be obtained.
- 💡 There is no first place, there is no last place. You have the same worth as everybody else.
- 💡 To yourself, in your own life, you need to be the most valuable person in the world.
- 💡 There is no one else with whom you will spend every single second of your life, other than you.
- 💡 There is nobody else who is in control of how you treat your body and of the choices you make to keep yourself safe and make your life beautiful. Only you.
- 💡 Nobody is going to give you self-worth. You have to decide to reach down and pick it up.

SELF-CARE

I bet you think you know what self-care is all about, don't you? It's candles and shit right? It is about having a bubble bath and painting your toenails and having a herbal tea. That's self-care. You do that a little bit every now and again when you remember.

No. That is not the self-care I am talking about. It is a part of it but it is a small part of it.

Self-care is about excessive kindness. Why do I say 'excessive'? I use that word because we all have a mindset block about being kind to ourselves. If I just said to you that self-care is being kind to yourself, you would go back to that original thought. You would give yourself a nice cup of tea and a sit down with your feet up, and you would think you had been kind to yourself. You would put some lavender drops in your bath and buy yourself some fluffy socks. Yet that is nowhere near enough. I have to say excessive kindness to get you past that mindset block about how we view being kind to ourselves so you can understand I want you to be kind to yourself, to care for yourself, the way that you care for other people. It is that level of care.

How do we care for the others in our lives whom we love? We talk kindly to them, and we know if ever we do not talk kindly to them, that is not showing them kindness and love. We are understanding and forgiving towards them. Yes, they have flaws, they have faults, they have their little quirks and triggers, we get that and we understand and we forgive. We show them love. These are the people in our lives and we show them that and we tell them that all the time. We recognise their needs, and we try to fulfil them. We look after them, from the basics of feeding our kids right up to understanding that our partner needs a little bit of quiet time and trying to make that happen. We try to fulfil the needs of the people in our lives whom we love. We might even adapt things to suit those needs. We might have people in our lives whom we love, who need a little bit of adaptation, for whom we need to do things slightly differently because of the way they are, what they need, what they like, what sets them off. So we adapt things for them. This is how we treat the people that we love.

Here is the tricky part: true self-care is about doing just that for yourself. Yeah. Sounds excessive, doesn't it? It is not – it shouldn't be, but that is why we say excessive kindness. True self-care is about being your own best friend, your own lover, your own parent, your own boss, your own cheerleader. Being all of those things to yourself. That is what self-care actually looks like. The phrase has become so over-used and so linked to all these things we can buy, it's a great marketing tool, we have forgotten that it is exactly what it says. It is caring for ourselves.

Let's think about positive self-talk, how we speak to

ourselves. How often do you talk kindly to yourself? How often do you talk unkindly to yourself? I hear so many people say, and they don't even realise they are doing it as it is such a habit, they say, 'Oh of course I'm rubbish at that', 'Oh sorry that sounds really bad doesn't it?', 'Oh I'm so bad at this', 'Yeah I'm really crap, I'm sorry'. All the time. That is their inner self-talk slipping out into their conversation. You can guarantee that if they are saying it out loud to me, they are saying it inside to themselves multiple times a day. *I am rubbish, I am crap at this, I am so bad, I am in the wrong* ... that is the self-talk.

Just imagine for a moment that you spoke to your child that way. That you spoke to your lover that way. That you told them, constantly, day-in and day-out how crap they are. It is hard to even think about treating someone that way, but we do it to ourselves all the time. Absolutely awful. It is the opposite of self-care – it is self-abuse. Positive self-talk can be about mantras and telling yourself you are the best, but actually it is about the inner monologue every day. We have to keep an eye on it. If you are not used to your inner self-talk being kind and forgiving and generous and encouraging, it takes practice.

You might want to start by doing it out loud. Not necessarily in the supermarket; people might think you are a bit of a loon if you are going around the store saying, 'I love you, I believe in you, you've got this, you can do this shopping trip!', but believe me, I have said it inside my own head on days when the grocery shop feels overwhelming! To start with, when you are alone, a little bit out loud can really help because it gets you hearing it. 'I love you.' Can you imagine if you said that to yourself? You say it to the people that you love every day. Not necessarily in a hugely emotional way, sometimes it is a throwaway as they leave the house, but you say it. 'I love you, have a good day.' 'I love you, goodnight.' Why don't we say it to ourselves like that? Just a little throwaway: 'Good morning self, love you, let's have a good one!'

It is the most important thing because that inner monologue is going to happen regardless, we cannot switch it off. If you do not concentrate on it being positive and kind and loving, it is going to be the other thing. It is going to be that horrible voice, following you around, that you cannot get away from, day-in and day-out telling you how shit you are. If you imagine doing that to somebody else, it is upsetting and hurtful and painful. Why do we do it to ourselves?

That is true self-care: being kind to ourselves inside our own heads.

Then there are outward things we can do to be kind to ourselves, material things, slightly more superficial things. We can give gifts to ourselves. I have come to the conclusion that the gifts we get from ourselves are actually really important. It started for me when I got divorced, just buying myself flowers every week. Not as a big gesture, just part of the grocery shop. I'd pop them in a vase and make sure I always had fresh flowers. I realised that I deserve flowers every week from myself. I love me, I'm quite fond of me really, why not get me some flowers to say well done. I realised gradually that this giving gifts to myself is important, partly because it is fantastic self-care but also because it really changes my perception of gifts from other people.

So often, if it is a big birthday or Christmas or something special like Mother's Day, as much as we don't like to think of ourselves as materialistic people, we see the gifts we receive as a demonstration of our worth, and sometimes we can be a bit disappointed. We don't like to admit it to ourselves, but when we don't quite get what we'd hoped for on Mother's Day, or not quite the Christmas present we had envisaged from our partner, we feel uncomfortable about being disappointed, but we are!

The answer is to give ourselves the gifts we know we want, we know we deserve, we are imagining would come from someone who really cares about us – because we really care about us! Do that for yourself. Do you know what happens when you do that? Gifts from other people then become the wonderful bonus that they should be. A wonderful gesture. Oh my goodness, they got me flowers, that is so kind, thank you! Rather than, 'Hmph, bloody hell, that's the first time in six months you've got me flowers, flipping heck!' – that kind of resentful feeling.

When you get yourself a Christmas stocking filled with the things you really want, the lovely things you are imagining, then whatever anyone else gets you becomes what it should be: a gift. Their thought. A lovely bonus. Rather than the only thing you get to demonstrate how much worth you have. You are doing that for yourself. Get yourself the birthday presents and the Christmas presents, the presents for every special occasion where you are secretly hoping that someone is going to spoil you – good lord, get yourself something for Valentine's Day! Care for yourself the way you want to be cared for. That reduces the resentment, and the disappointment, and the guilt that comes with having them both.

We know how we want to be cared for, and then we wait for somebody else to do it. Yet we know how to do it best! Nobody else is going to hit that right, not unless you give them a literal shopping list and that doesn't feel good, does it? What is the point of that? Do it for yourself. Gift giving for yourself is really good self-care.

Mindset Block Alert!

I find it really hard to love myself.

Just note it down, that loving yourself, caring for yourself the way you care for others feels beyond weird, it feels wrong or scary. Note it down and remember it is something to look at or tackle in some way.

I had to learn to frequently tell my children I love them because that wasn't the norm in my house growing up, the actual saying of it. Now, ten years on from when I started parenting, it is just habit, I don't even think about it. I tell them I love them when I say goodnight and throughout the day whenever it feels appropriate. I did have to practise though, I had to remind myself to say it at bedtime every night, even if I didn't remember at any other time. Now it has become second nature. It is the same with caring for ourselves. If it doesn't come naturally at first, make it a practice. Make it a practice that is going to become second nature, and that you are going to learn how to care for yourself the way you care for others.

Guess what? When you do this, it means that no matter what happens to you in life, you will always have your best friend, your lover, your parent, your boss and your best supporter with you, no matter what happens, because that person is you. That is truly self-care.

Thinking Points

- Self-care is about treating yourself with excessive kindness.
- I want you to be kind to yourself, to care for yourself, the way that you care for other people.
- True self-care is about being your own best friend, your own lover, your own parent, your own boss, your own cheerleader. Being all of those things to yourself.
- True self-care is being kind to yourself inside your own head.
- Care for yourself the way that you want to be cared for.

NEEDS AND REWARDS

Unmet needs lead to a lack of productivity, feelings of overwhelm and burnout. That is the reality. We all think we know what we need – food, water, shelter right? Yet those are just our most basic of needs. Our 'physiological needs' on Maslow's hierarchy:

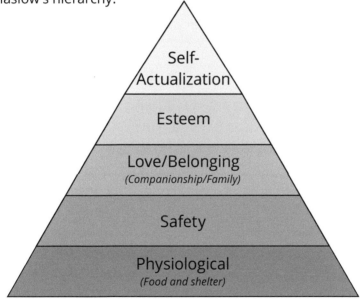

[credit: https://www.princetonpolicy.com/ppa-blog/
2018/5/21/a-conservative-hierarchy-of-needs]

We all have more complex needs than that, and they are vitally important in our quest to get the most we can out of life.

The trouble is, before we can consistently meet those needs, we often need to forgive ourselves for having them. We look at things like Maslow's hierarchy and we think, *Oh yes, that makes sense*, but we find it hard to apply it to ourselves. *Sorry, no time for 'self-actualisation', I've got two kids and a business to run*. It becomes almost a badge of honour that we don't meet our needs. This has got to stop.

If we are surrounded by people who act as though it's admirable that they barely have time in their day to have a wee and hydrate themselves, we start to believe that this is the benchmark. 'How many of your needs did you ignore today? Oh, you haven't slept well and you missed lunch? Wow, you must be really amazing!' Our perception of success has somehow got all out of whack, and we imagine that 'powering on through' is the route to greatness. Why is this?

The answer actually lies in Maslow's hierarchy itself. It is important to all of us that we feel safe, and, for many people, having the self-worth to recognise that our needs are actually vitally important just does not feel safe. Meeting our needs – the basic and the complex – feels selfish and self-centred and that does not feel safe; we will get into trouble for that. Somewhere along the path of our lives we have been taught it is wrong to value ourselves enough to prioritise our own needs, desires and requirements.

Then there is also that need to belong. If everyone around us is acting as though being too busy to take a break is somehow impressive, we will want to act that way too. We want to belong in the group; we don't want to be different because that would make us an outsider.

My advice? Find a different group.

Your needs are of vital importance for these two reasons: you have enormous value and you deserve to have all of the things that you need, and consistently meeting those needs will make it possible for you to perform at your best, in all areas of life.

So, let's get real and talk about my needs so you can see exactly what I'm talking about. I nailed down my list a couple of years ago, and whenever I'm feeling a bit 'off' I go down the list and circle the needs that I haven't met that day or that week. Meeting those needs almost always solves the problem. This is my list. Yours will be unique to you:

In no particular order, I need: water, music & dancing, fresh air & sunshine, orgasms, a stretched & exercised body, to get out in my car, healthy food, to feel safe, coffee, to care for my children the best I can, to feel productive, hot showers, rest, human connection, a beautiful home environment and freedom.

I realised that caring for my children the best I can is a need. I feel uncomfortable if I feel I haven't done my best job there. It is not a value or a desire or a wish. It is a need. I have to be the best parent I can be, it's part of my bedrock.

Being a good parent does not mean, however, that I put my needs aside. Far from it. When you parent alone you do not have the luxury of being able to run yourself into the ground knowing someone else will pick up when you collapse. You have to be able to perform well the whole time the children are with you (their dad and I split the week 50:50). Like an athlete planning a race, you can't give it your all at the start and then have nothing left to give. You have to pace yourself and carefully look after your needs.

It is the same with running a business. Pushing yourself to burnout might be very 'impressive' in some circles, but it's not a long-term plan. If you are serious about building a business, you are in it for the long haul, and you won't be able to keep up business growth and performance if you run yourself into the ground. You cannot afford to ignore your own needs. Meeting them is what keeps you performing at your best.

So here is my real talk about our needs: find yourself a social and/or business group where meeting your needs is valued rather than it being a badge of honour to always be exhausted and depleted. Recognise your value and how you bring far more to the world if you are performing at your best. Recognise how privileged we are to have the opportunity to meet our needs when many in the world cannot. Do not dismiss that opportunity.

Yet even meeting our needs is not enough. We also need to reward ourselves at appropriate junctures.

A friend of mine went through something really difficult recently that had been looming for some time, and she got through it well with the best possible outcome. So I asked her how she would be rewarding herself?

Inevitably she had not thought about it but, fortunately, I was able to persuade her that a reward was necessary, even if it was just a bar of chocolate. 'Reward yourself!' I said. 'No one else will. It's no good waiting for the universe to do it.'

Why is rewarding ourselves so important, apart from the fact that it's an act of self love we all deserve? Well, it's all about balance.

When you mess something up, make a mistake, embarrass yourself or upset somebody, how long do you berate yourself for that? How much time do you spend cringing, and worrying, and making amends or apologising? How much time do you spend beating yourself up and feeling horrible about yourself?

All of that needs to be balanced out by rewards. Our brains focus on what we feed them, so if we focus hard on the cock-ups but ignore the triumphs, our brains will conclude that our life is mostly cock-ups and will deliver our self-esteem accordingly.

In one of my Facebook groups, we have a weekly thread celebrating our 'wins' and one of my clients said that she would feel uncomfortable posting on it because talking about her achievements felt weird; she had not been brought up that way. We discussed how never mentioning successes but focusing on anything that goes wrong will give her brain the impression that things are a disaster, or that, at best, she is hanging on by a thread, when the truth is she is an immensely successful business woman who has grown her business through a global pandemic.

Rudyard Kipling says in his poem *If* that we should

meet with triumph and disaster
And treat those two impostors just the same.

That kind of stoicism may indeed be desirable, but most of us find it almost impossible to meet disaster with equanimity. If that is the case, we need to make as big a fuss about triumphs, if not bigger, as we do about disaster in order to balance the scales and keep ourselves rooted in reality. If we do that, we may not be following the spirit of Kipling's message, but at least we are treating the two things just the same...

Celebrating our wins and rewarding ourselves is not being arrogant, attention-seeking, being 'big-headed' or whatever other unhelpful messages we learned in our childhood. Quite the opposite: it is helping us to keep it real. The story that we are hopeless, imposters, struggling and so on, that is the story to be scoffed at. If we balance that story with a recognition of our wins, and a conscious effort to reward ourselves for them, we will maintain a more realistic picture of who we are: imperfect human beings who are capable of making mistakes and achieving things, regularly, within the same lifetime.

So next time you feel as though celebrating a success is an uncomfortable thing to do, remember you have two sensible choices: celebrate the wins, or ignore the mistakes. Either of those will create balance. Sweat the mistakes and ignore the achievements? Your view of yourself will be an unhelpful untruth.

Thinking Points

- Unmet needs lead to a lack of productivity, feelings of overwhelm and burnout.
- Forgive yourself for having needs.
- Consistently meeting those needs will make it possible for you to perform at your best, in all areas of life.
- You cannot afford to ignore your own needs. Meeting them is what keeps you performing at your best.
- If you balance the negative stories with a recognition of your wins, and make a conscious effort to reward yourself for them, you will maintain a more realistic picture of who you are.

BEING THE BEST BOSS

As business owners, we can use the phrase 'I am my own boss'. To people in employment, that might sound like wonderful freedom, which, of course, it is but only if we take some time to consider what kind of boss we actually want to be.

Being your own boss is freeing – you can set your own hours, set your own expectations, choose your own rewards – but most of us pretty quickly realise that doing exactly what we like comes with some clear constraints because, of course, we need to do what is best for the business. Or else we will not have a business to run. So there are certain things that we have to do.

Yet we often miss out a key part of being a small business owner, of being our own boss. We know that we have to be our own finance department, our own marketing department, our own operations manager, we understand that. We forget, though, that we also have to be our own HR department. Do you think that you do not need to consider your human resources or people management just because you work alone? Sorry. You really do!

Often people are self-employed because they did not have a great experience in employment. Which leaves them thinking, *I hate bosses, I don't want to be the boss, I don't even like that word!*

Mindset Block Alert!

I don't like what I picture when I hear the word 'boss' – I don't want to see myself that way.

What does 'boss' really mean? It simply means the person who makes the decisions, the person with whom the buck stops. That is all. There is no rule that you have to wear a pinstripe suit and become an asshole. That is not a requirement of being a boss! You just have to be the decision maker, that is all.

You are your own boss, but you are also your own employee. That comes with certain responsibilities around how you treat yourself. What kind of boss are you? Are you the best boss with the best management style, or are you some rotten old tyrant for whom nobody would ever work? Is that how you treat yourself?

Consider these questions:

*   What hours do you expect yourself to keep?
*   Do you get annoyed with yourself if you do not work evenings and weekends?
*   How do you reward yourself for a job well done?
*   How do you motivate yourself to do your best?
*   How do you handle things when you make a mistake?

What kind of a boss are you to yourself?

We have all had frustrating managers, and we all know what team leadership looks like when it's good and when it sucks. Becoming self-employed we think to ourselves, *Hooray, I am free of all that rubbish!* but then what do we do? We take on the worst traits of every bad boss we have ever had, and we treat ourselves like crap.

This is a problem for two reasons. The biggest reason is because it makes you miserable when your boss (you) is constantly mean to you. I am sure none of us sets out to be miserable in our working lives, so it is a pretty big problem if you then become that terrible boss to yourself, with ridiculous expectations, never saying thank you, never rewarding good performance, always having a go at yourself, always having a gripe. You did not go into business with yourself to have that boss and feel miserable!

The other reason it is a real problem if you become that boss to yourself is that it sets the pattern for the management style you are going to have. If in the future you take on freelancers, sub-contractors or employees, you are going to find it hard to treat them any better than you treat yourself. Rightly so! Why should they get treated any better than you do? You are the one who has built this business. What do we get in those circumstances? Resentment.

I see it often: business owners who treat themselves really poorly, who are dreadful bosses to themselves, expecting way more of themselves than they would ever expect from anyone else, who forget to reward themselves. Suddenly these business owners have a team, and they know they have to manage that team. They recognise that they cannot constantly yell at their team or expect them to work weekends. They have to say thank you and give their team a little prize or a bonus when they do well, and the resentment becomes huge. That business owner starts to think, *Wow, I don't get any of that, and these people are not even running the business, they don't put the work in yet I have to say thank you and give them a pat on the head. I don't get that, do I!* Yet whose fault is that? That is where resentment comes in very strongly, when you are not being as good a boss to yourself as you are trying to be to your team.

The place to nip that in the bud is before you get any team members. Right now, think about what kind of boss you want to be to yourself, and then to everybody else.

Before you start another working day with the worst boss in the world, grab a piece of paper and write down the answers to these questions:

* What can I reasonably expect of myself?
* What is a compassionate and productive way to deal with mistakes when I make them?
* What do I need from myself in order to feel motivated?
* What is the reward structure that I have in place for myself?

This is writing your employee handbook – for yourself. You do need an employee handbook – for you. Even if you never take on any team members, you need to have the answers to these questions set out for yourself. If you have never thought about the answers to those questions, chances are you are working yourself into the ground, berating yourself horribly every time you make a mistake. You are never really motivating yourself because you expect yourself to just be 'on it' every day. I bet you are not rewarding yourself. You are paying yourself, sure, but that's just what you get for doing the job. What about when things go really well? What about when you get that new client or you make it through that presentation or you deal with a mistake really well? How do you reward yourself?

Nobody else is going to be cracking open the champagne for you.

I once worked in a law firm and when a big deal was closed there would be champagne on a Friday afternoon, provided by the partners. When you work for yourself, nobody is giving you that unless you give it to yourself. You are your own boss. That means you set the tone for every working day, and you create your working environment. It is you, and you alone, who decides on the expectations. Nobody else is going to give you a day off when you need one. No one is going to give you permission, no one is going to remind you that you have not taken your holiday allowance for the year. You have to do that for yourself.

Have you even considered how much holiday you expect yourself to take on an annual basis? Have you written that down anywhere?

Nobody else is going to give you a Christmas bonus. All of these things are down to you now. How do you want to treat yourself? What kind of boss do you actually want to be?

This is one of the reasons why we have already looked at self-belief, self-worth and self-care. There is nobody else who is going to do this management stuff for you anymore, it is down to you. You need to treat yourself as a valued employee. No one is going to give you permission. No one will phone you on a Friday and say, 'Well done, you've smashed it this week, go home early'. If we are lucky, we have had managers who do that kind of thing, but as business owners we have to do that for ourselves or it will not happen.

Do you give yourself time in lieu? We all have busy, complicated lives and we rarely work 9 to 5. Of course we work weekends. I am writing this on a Sunday! That doesn't mean, though, that we have to work all hours God sends. We can take time off whenever we like as well as work whenever we like. That is the flip side of flexibility. If you work in the evenings when the kids are in bed, do you then give yourself some time off in the middle of the day to go for a walk? Or do you imagine you 'should' be working because it is normal 'office hours' at that point? You set your own hours now. What are your expectations for yourself? How many hours do you expect yourself to work per week? What do you do with the time that is outside those hours? Do you expect yourself to just keep going? If you do, I will tell you what will happen: you will start to hate it, and you will burn out. If you were an employee, you would leave the job, but you cannot leave because it is your business. So you are going to get yourself into a right pickle!

Think about the long term. I do not think many of us went into business to do it for a year and then burn out, hate it and give up to do something else. Most of us went into business because this is what we want to do now, so we have to make is sustainable. We are talking here about long-term strategy, keeping you performing well in your business. In order to get the most out of yourself, you need to be a good boss to yourself. Otherwise, you are going to feel exhausted and demotivated, your self-talk will deteriorate and if you ever do get team members, you are not going to be a good manager to them, either.

You will look back and wonder where it all went wrong, and it is because you are waiting for somebody else to tell you how to reward yourself and how to treat yourself. Nobody will. You are your own boss: it is down to you now.

Before you start another working day as the downtrodden employee of a mean, demanding and uncompromising boss, I suggest you take some time to consider whether or not that is the boss you want to be, and whether it is the boss you want to work for. I suggest you be the best boss you can to yourself as well as the best owner for your business. You, as your employee, deserve that.

Thinking Points

- ♀ What is your employee handbook for yourself?
- ♀ What kind of a boss do you want to be?
- ♀ You need to treat yourself as a valued employee. No one is going to give you permission.
- ♀ In order to get the most out of yourself you need to be a good boss to yourself.

LEADERSHIP

Leadership is important in lots of walks of life, and, of course, it is important if you are thinking of ever expanding your business and bringing people into your team. It is also important if you are part of any kind of group. You might not be *the* leader, but at times you may be called upon to be *a* leader. If you are already thinking, *I do not see myself as a leader, I don't do leadership!* that's okay, but sometimes you are going to be the leader. Even if it is at your child's birthday party, somebody has to be in charge, right? There are always going to be times when leadership is thrust upon you, even if it is not something you are considering for your business.

If you are thinking of ever bringing people into your business, leadership is an important element of that.

We have looked at what it means to be the boss and what it does not mean. It does not mean that you have to be the one in the hat with the whistle, the Scout leader, the one waving an umbrella in the front like the tour guide – there is no requirement for you to have any particular personality or any particular kind of clothing in order to be a leader. Notice if you are already thinking in stereotypes, because if you are ever called upon to be a leader, you will still be you.

What it means to be a leader of a business is that the buck stops with you. This is your business, these are your decisions to make. You are probably going to be the one who reaps the most benefit, certainly long term, from the business because you have built it and you are taking it in the direction that you choose to reach the goals that you have set. You are the one in charge because you have set that course.

Please forgive me – I love an extended metaphor, and in this chapter you are coming with me onto our ship. Think *Pirates of the Caribbean*! We are steering our ship. Sometimes we can get caught up in thinking about the other people in our team, the customers, everyone else connected to the business, and whilst all of those people are vitally important, as the captain of this ship you are the one responsible for everybody's well-being and for everybody getting out of it what they need. You are responsible for making sure that everything is working properly, and if it is not and there is a problem, no matter who or what causes that problem, it is your responsibility. You might not be the one to actually get your hands dirty and fix it, you might delegate that, but it is your responsibility, and if it does not get fixed, the buck stops with you.

You are also the one who is setting the course. You are the one who has decided in which direction this ship is going. You are the one who knows where you are headed and why. You are making decisions based on that plan, and not everybody in your team is going to fully understand that plan. Even if they might be a whizz at their area of the business and they are telling you what they need, nobody knows the whole business and the whole plan better than you do.

What does all of this mean? It means that there are certain things that you deserve because of the responsibilities you are taking on. I say deserve because one of the things people get hugely caught up in, the moment they imagine being a leader, is worrying about how they are going to be perceived. *Are people going to like me? Am I going to be a good leader or am I going to upset people?* Of course, none of us goes out there wanting to upset people, thinking it does not matter if we trample all over everybody else. Yet you deserve to have your plan and your requirements respected because it is your ship and your course.

It is not about everybody being equal and everybody getting along. It is great when everybody gets along, and we will be talking about team management in the next chapter. At the end of the day, though, it is your ship, and people are going to come and go.

What do people need from their leader? We can get very caught up in thinking that we want to be liked and that we want to be nice. Such an awful word, 'nice'. That is not actually helpful when you are in a leadership position. This is not an equal relationship. This is a relationship where you are the one in charge. In order to fulfil the plan that you have set out, people need to be on board with it. Good leadership involves discussion, listening, assisting and training, but at the end of the day if somebody is not into that plan and coming along with that plan, they can go and get their own ship.

We are not trying to be friends. We can be friendly, but we

are not trying to be friends. Friendship is a balance of power, something equal: at times you need your friend, at other times they need you, you give and they give and there is a nice balance. When that balance is out of whack sometimes the friendship feels a bit uncomfortable. Whereas in a leadership position, you are always going to be the one in the position of power.

Mindset Block Alert!

Power and decision making, being in charge, make me feel like I'm being unpleasant.

So often we have had people in those positions of power over us who have misused that power and been unpleasant. We are not talking about being nasty. We are talking about having boundaries because you know that the important thing is keeping this ship on course.

What do I mean by boundaries? Let us say that somebody in your team comes to you and they have an ambition. They tell you they would really love to retrain in a different pro-fession and, therefore, they are going to need flexible hours to accommodate their training and fulfil their dream. If you were their friend, you would tell them it sounds amazing and you would encourage them to follow their dream. As the leader of your business, your first thought needs to be about what this means for the business. If there is a way to make it work for the business, and if there is going to be a benefit to the business, then go for it. Help to facilitate their dream, be flexible, come up with a creative solution. If, however, it is going to be detrimental to the business and it is going to knock your ship off course, you are under no obligation to be a nice friend and agree to their request. It is not your responsibility to be the encouraging friend to your team members – they will have friends to do that for them. It is your responsibility to tell them that, whilst their plan sounds amazing, you cannot see a way to make it work for the business. Explain the way it could work for the business, and if that does not work for them they will have to consider leaving the business. You can tell them you value them and you would miss them, but it is their decision, and you have to make the decisions that are best for the business.

It is not about being 'mean' or obstructive. It is the difference between being the captain of a ship, the leader of a business, and being a friend. It is a different role.

This can be very challenging because there will have been times in our lives when we have had people in charge of us who have not been pleasant, and this can get into some fairly deep stuff, as the people we start off having in charge of us in life are, of course, our parents. If we have been parented in a way that doesn't feel like leadership and feels more like authoritarian awfulness, we may not have a good model of what leadership can look like. Leadership, in a lot of ways, is similar to good parenting. People don't necessarily want their leader to be super friendly and 'nice'. We do not want people to be unpleasant to us, but if someone is in charge and therefore has an element of control over us, what we really need them to provide is emotional safety. We need clarity. We need boundaries. We need to know what we are allowed to do and what we are not allowed to do. What we are encouraged to do, what we are asked not to do. How we can succeed, what success looks like, how we can impress, and where we might go wrong.

We need that clarity way more than we need friendly and nice. If we are in a team, the leader does have some power, and taken to extremes, it can be frightening when someone has power over you, and decision-making power over you. To be a good leader you need to demonstrate that you will use that power wisely, and ensure that everybody knows where the lines are. It is far more important to be clear about your expectations.

What if it goes wrong? What does it going wrong look like to you? If you are being clear, if you have good boundaries, if you are being kind and you are listening, but somebody suddenly flies off the handle, tells you that you are a horrible person and they hate working for you, that is not a rational response from them. If that did happen, that is more about them and not a sudden signal that you have been a terrible leader. In reality though, outside of our worst fears, what is more likely to happen is that sometimes people will come to you with problems. They will tell you there is a part of the job they do not really enjoy, for example. That is not it all going horribly wrong. That is not a catastrophe. That is an opportunity to have a discussion to find out how you can help them, and whether or not you can help them in a way that supports the business, or whether they need to help themselves by moving outside of the business.

It going 'horribly wrong' very suddenly is rare in a well-led group or organisation. It is far more likely that you are simply going to have conversations, which we are all perfectly capable of having.

Your measure of success as a leader is not whether everybody likes you, it is whether you are retaining people who benefit your business. Are those people staying with you? If the people who benefit your business leave the team, is that because of something you did not provide? If it is due to decisions you made, are you happy with those decisions? Did they want a pay rise you just could not facilitate for example? Are you keeping the people you want to keep, and if they are leaving, are you content with the reasons they left?

If you are retaining the team members you want to retain, it does not matter whether you are nice or kind or friendly or everybody likes you, because clearly you are a good leader. They are staying.

Thinking Points

- As a business owner, you are the one in charge because you have set the course.
- Leadership means bringing together everyone's priorities and concerns and focusing them on the big picture that to start with only you can see.
- You deserve to have your plan and your requirements respected because it is your business and your plan.
- Being a leader is to be in a position of power **but** that power does not have to be abused.

- 💡 Don't let your experiences of poor leadership put you off taking on a leadership role – you can choose to do it well!
- 💡 Good leaders provide clarity and boundaries, which makes their team feel safe.
- 💡 Your measure of success as a leader is whether you are retaining people who are of benefit to your business.

TEAM MANAGEMENT

You may only have a small team, but this is relevant no matter what size of team you have.

As a small business owner, maybe you work twelve hours a day on your business, you are constantly thinking about ways to improve things. You find it hard to switch off at the weekends, and getting a new client is cause for huge celebration. So why do your team not seem to give a shit? Firstly, if that sounds like you in terms of how hard you are pushing yourself, you need to go back a couple of chapters and think about being the best boss to yourself, but this is a common problem. As a business owner you are always going to be the person who is passionately involved in business development, progress, quality, and when it is like that for you as the person who has built the business, you can sometimes be at a bit of a loss as to why your team does not seem to have the same dedication.

The truth is, nobody working in your business is ever going to care about it as much as you do, and it is unfair to expect that of them. You can bring from them the dedication and commitment that you need, though, in two ways: by being clear about your expectations, and by being clear about rewards and consequences.

As a driven, ambitious business owner it might be painfully obvious to you that somebody should just do their best all of the time – strive to get it right and never settle for less. That is who you are: you set up your own business, that is your mindset in life and you have to feel like that to be the kind of person who is going to start up alone. Your team members are going to have their own priorities, their own ambitions and their own things that motivate them, plus their own view on what 'best' looks like. It might not chime with your view. These people are individuals with their own lives, and they are not necessarily going to see things the way you do. Even if they do, it is not their business, so their priorities are inevitably going to be slightly different.

What you need to do is ensure that they are working in a way that works for your business. In order to achieve that, there needs to be clarity on certain things.

* What are the business values?
* What does good customer service look like?
* What do you want team members to avoid doing?
* What should they do if there is a problem?
* What is definitely unacceptable behaviour?

These things should be really clear to all of your team members, and if they are not, you are probably going to run across some trouble.

For my team at Clear Day, our business values are calm, clarity, confidence, focus and progress. My team know that good customer service looks like bringing calm to a client's day, making them feel confident in our ability to solve their problems, and clearing their day so they can make progress in their business. I tell all of my team members that what we want to avoid is taking any kind of panic or chaos to the client. Amongst ourselves we might have a flap about what is happening or get frustrated and lose the plot somewhat, but the client does not need to see any of that or have it brought to their day. My team know that if they have a problem, they come to me rather than putting that problem into the lap of the client. I am very clear about what is unacceptable: for me it is unacceptable if there is an issue that I do not get told about upfront. Any problem that occurs, we can deal with, but I do not want to find out there has been a problem I was unaware of and now it has escalated because it has been left. Not bringing problems to me when they first arise is unacceptable.

Is that the kind of clarity that you are providing to your team? If not, the question is how does your team know how to do a good job for you? Most people do actually want to do their best. If they do not know what 'best' looks like to you, though, then that is an almost impossible challenge. I know what 'best' looks like is really obvious to you, but it will not be obvious to them – everybody has a different view on what best, finished and acceptable look like. So make those things really clear. When your team members have their own lives, priorities and incomes to worry about, they will appreciate that clarity.

Make sure that your expectations are clearly recorded somewhere, no matter how small your team. Somewhere in writing, ideally, so it can be referred to, even if it is just a starred message in a WhatsApp group. Give people the opportunity to do their best for you by telling them what best looks like.

When they meet or exceed those expectations, remember to say thank you. Which brings us on to rewards and consequences.

Some people are motivated purely by the knowledge of a job well done. Some people are not. You want to make sure that you can get the best out of everybody, and the way to do that is to have in place some rewards and some consequences, however simple. This does not have to be anything complicated. Most small businesses cannot afford staff bonuses on a regular basis, and very few employers want to be going down the route of formal grievance processes every time someone messes up – it is a waste of everybody's time and it is often not appropriate to escalate things to that level. There are far simpler ways of achieving better team performance.

What can rewards look like? Saying thank you and well done is the first thing, which often gets missed. Have you said that to someone, and, if appropriate, have you done that in front of the rest of the team? A bottle of wine for someone who performed really well on a certain task, a box of chocolates for the person who first hit their target. A social media post celebrating someone in your team who has gone the extra mile. Certainly, passing on good client feedback to the team members who helped with the project. As business owners we are responsible for managing the negative feedback, but we are also the ones who see the positive feedback, and it is really important to remember to pass that on to anyone who was responsible for making that feedback happen.

Replying to client feedback by copying in the relevant team members rather than taking all of the credit for yourself can be another reward.

On the other side of the coin we have consequences, and they do not have to be anything enormous, either. It could be something like a phone call to ask what went wrong. An email asking for three learning points that the team member is going to take forward to ensure that the mistake does not happen again. Perhaps more regular one-to-one catch-ups with a particular team member to try to get to the root of a problem; a focused chat with somebody to find out if they are unhappy, to find out if something is happening that you need to know about.

These things do not sound like punishments, and they are not supposed to. Consequences are not intended to shame and punish, they are there to make it clear when something is a problem and to try to ensure that the problem does not arise again. It is about getting to the root of the problem, not shaming the person. Nobody performs better when they are mentally beaten down. If you think of consequences as a stick with which to beat someone, that is not going to be helpful. Consequences are a way of shedding light on a situation, pro- viding some clarity so you are not all fumbling around in the dark trying to figure out what went wrong and how to fix it.

In the same way, rewards are not pats on the head. You are not infantilising your team: you are making clear that you appreciate their efforts and you understand that they are adults whose focus and time are valuable, so you appreciate that they have put their focus and time into your business.

When the only reward that people get is payment, they are going to do the bare minimum to ensure they get paid. Not everybody, but most people. That is logical and does not make them bad people – they have their own issues to tackle. When the only consequence is you, as the business owner, clearing up the mess, nobody is going to bother avoiding a similar problem in the future. Without any consequence, they may not even recognise there was a problem in the first place. It may feel easy to fix things yourself, but there needs to be recognition that something happened that should be avoided in the future.

 *Mindset Block Alert!*

I understand rewarding my team and there being consequences for them as well, but I cannot imagine including myself in that.

It is important to be clear about what will happen when things go well and when things go badly.

We all understand rewarding ourselves, even if we might not do it we understand the concept. What about the concept of consequences when we make a mistake? Everything you have just read goes out of the window and you are likely going back to the idea of a stick with which to beat yourself, but that is not the answer. When you make a mistake, do the same things for yourself as we have talked about doing with your team. Check in with yourself. Are you doing okay? How can that issue be avoided in the future, but also, is there a reason that mistake happened? Are you exhausted? Is there something you are not enjoying? Do you need some help? Are you okay? A consequence is something that happens because a mistake has happened, not a punishment.

When something goes right, you need to be buying yourself that bottle of wine or that box of chocolates or whatever the appropriate reward might be.

Be as clear as you can be, and we have already discussed how leadership is about providing clarity because that makes people feel safe. When they know where the boundaries are, that makes them feel safe, and people who feel safe perform better and feel happier.

It is not about being everybody's best friend. It is about ensuring that everyone knows how they can do their best and that they are going to get rewarded for doing their best. In a team situation, that is what people want. To know that their best efforts are going to be recognised and it is worth them making those efforts. As a business owner, that is what you want: for people to be putting in their best efforts whenever they can.

Thinking Points

💡 No one will ever care about your business as much as you do, but there are ways to motivate and reward team members so that you get the best from them.

- ♀ Be clear with your team about your expectations and what success looks like to you.
- ♀ Rewards and consequences are vital – and neither has to be big or dramatic.
- ♀ Be sure to include yourself in both the rewards and the consequences and remember – consequences are not about punishment!

WORK–LIFE BALANCE

Work-life balance. A familiar phrase, but an odd thought. The idea that we have work and then we have life ... what does that even mean? Let us work out what it is that we are trying to balance. The idea that we have work on one side of the scales, life on the other side and somehow we are trying to create a 50:50 split so that the scales are balanced seems very strange to me. For most of us, work is an important part of life, it is not separate to life, and we have a heck of a lot to fit in to the 'life' side that is not work, and it does not function as a 50:50 split.

The idea of 50 per cent work, 50 per cent life is an old-fashioned way of looking at work, and I suspect if it was ever true, it was only true for people who just did paid work and then relaxed. They did not have any other commitments. Which I am pretty sure is none of us!

So let's talk about our kind of work-life balance and what we are actually trying to balance. We have our paid work, if we do some, which usually takes up a good chunk of most people's week. We might have some voluntary or community work, commitments at our children's school, additional unpaid obligations of some description. Then there is parenting for a lot of us, which is not something that you switch on and off: it is 24/7 even though the children may not always be with us. Whether or not we have children, we may have other family members for whom we are caring, or other people we have to fit into our week, in some fashion. Then we might have a romantic intimate relationship we are trying to spend some time on because those relationships don't just run themselves – they do need a little time spent on them. We have our friendships, which should not be hard work but we do need to spend a little time on them and indeed we like spending time on them!

Are you feeling exhausted at that list? We have not yet even got to the bit that everyone dreams about and plans, which are the things we actually enjoy. I may have already mentioned some of them, a lot of the things we mentioned above you may enjoy, which is good! Yet there are also the things we enjoy just for ourselves, and by ourselves. Hobbies, classes, exercise, things we do in our free time, things we do with our 'me' time. Ways we relax, including staring at the TV not speaking whilst watching back-to-back trash. Sleep – a very important thing we have to fit in every day! – and other forms of rest.

As you can see, there is no way that it is a set of scales with one thing on one side and one thing on the other. That is nonsense. It can feel like a juggling act; it can feel like spinning plates. What it is is deciding. It is not about balancing the scales, it is about deciding, and those decisions will be different for all of us. The questions to ask yourself are:

* What do you want more of?
* What do you want less of?

I cannot answer these questions for you. These decisions are different for everybody, but I would urge you to realise that it is for you to decide. The time to do the things that you actually enjoy and that bring you happiness, that time is not going to be given to you by anybody else. If you are spending every week or every month or every year waiting for little bits of time to crop up where you can sneak in a walk or a nap or a shopping trip or whatever you might want to enjoy, it is not going to be very well balanced.

If we go back to the idea of scales, in truth, one side is everything you feel obligated to do, and one side is everything you want to do. I suspect the obligations side is currently heavily weighed down. Obligations vs desires is a more appropriate balance to consider.

When we decide to have more of what we want in our days, weeks, months, schedules, what is it that is getting in the way of us just going for it? The first thing that springs to mind is often other people. We imagine that other people will object and have opinions, they will make it difficult, they will not want us to do more of the things we enjoy. That is something to look at. No matter who those people are – clients, family members, friends, partners – if they genuinely do not want us to do more of the things we enjoy, that is a problem. It is so easy to blame other people and say they will never stand for or accept something. Of course, we have to live our lives bearing in mind other people's needs, but the idea that they are going to object to us enjoying our time a little bit more? We need to look that full in the face and consider are they the kinds of people we want to be expending energy on, or consider whether we are being fair to them? Have we actually asked them or are we assuming their reaction?

Mindset Block Alert!

I don't feel as though I'm allowed to enjoy myself right now.

This block goes back to a very traditional model of life. Perhaps we all have it in the back of our minds, even though I am not convinced it exists for many people anymore. That model is:

* childhood and education
* work and/or parenting
* retirement
* death.

The time for enjoying life and reaping the benefits in this model is in retirement, which, firstly, seems depressing as we only get to enjoy life at the end. Secondly, real talk, we have absolutely no guarantee we are going to reach that point. We certainly have no guarantee that we are going to be healthy when we retire or that we are still going to be able to do all of the things we can do now. We have no clue what the future holds – which can be exciting or terrifying. All we know is what we have right now, and the opportunities that we have right now, and what we are capable of doing right now.

What do we want to do and how are we going to make that happen? We always imagine that the reward comes at the end, not just at the end of working life at retirement but also at the end of the day. We flop down on the sofa at the end of the day if the kids have gone to bed on time and we are lucky enough to get an hour in front of the TV, and that is our reward. Why? Why cannot we take the rewards at a different time of the day, when we are not exhausted? There might be opportunities at other times in the day that are not just vegging out in front of the TV with a box of chocolates. Why not take the rewards when we want to take them? When they fit in with how we actually want to live our lives?

Why would you not do that? What is the mindset block that is getting in the way of you saying to yourself, *I want more of this. I am going to rearrange my schedule so that it happens. I am going to ask the people around me for help if I need to, and I am going to trust that they care about me. I am going to actually enjoy life on a regular basis*. What is getting in the way of that? Is it something you need to work on or something with which another person needs to help?

The real balance is not between work and life. The real balance is between the negatives and the positives. Everything that we do: paid work, parenting, volunteering, relationships, everything has its positives and negatives. We want to balance out the frustration, the exhaustion, the anxiety and the busyness with enjoyment, joy, contentment and peace.

So often what we do in our downtime is really just a way

of numbing ourselves to the negatives. We just want some-thing that is going to enable us to switch off for two minutes because we are so tired of the negatives that we do not want to think anymore. That is not relaxation and enjoyment. That is where we need to be balancing. If your scales are tipped way down towards busyness and exhaustion and worry and franticness, we really need to think about how we can put some more things on the enjoyment and joy and contentment side of your scales. That is the balance that matters.

It is not about how many things we have going on. It is about which of them are obligations and which of them are things we desire.

Thinking Points

- ♀ We are all juggling an exhausting list of obligations – it is not about balancing two things on a set of scales.
- ♀ What do you want more of? What do you want less of? Those are the crucial questions.
- ♀ The real balance is between obligations and desires.
- ♀ We can take the rewards of life at any time – not just when something is completed.
- ♀ Can you be honest about who or what is stopping you from doing that?

PARENTING

Do not worry, I am not about to give you parenting tips! That is a whole bag of tricks I am not going anywhere near, and I am no more qualified to parent than is anyone else. So many business owners are also parents; indeed, needing flexibility of hours as a parent is often the reason people become self-employed. This chapter is not your guide to how to parent – this is your no bullshit guide to the experience of parenting.

I will start by telling you something that people seem to miss: parenting is a job. Like any other job, we choose it for its rewards, but it is not something we should be expecting to constantly love. No matter how much you love your job, you would not expect to enjoy every second of it. Like any other job, parenting can be rewarding, fulfilling, educational, exciting, hilarious, it is certainly an opportunity for personal growth. The benefits are huge. Yet like any other job, parenting is also frustrating, exhausting, worrying, anxiety-provoking, sometimes demoralising. It makes us question ourselves, it prods at our insecurities ... it is all the things that any other job is.

With how we approach parenting and how we think about the way it fits into our lives, we often miss that it is a job. Especially when we think about how we feel we 'should' be thinking about it or how we imagine other people think about it. The difficulty with parenting, of course, is that we cannot just leave the job in the office. There are lots of paid jobs where that is also a factor; we understand the idea of somebody not being able to switch off from work if they are doing something highly pressured. If they are working in the emergency services and they bring home worries and concerns about difficult things they have had to deal with. People working a 9 to 5 office job sometimes find it hard to switch off because they have been doing it all day and it is hard to change gears. We understand that, and we understand that not being able to switch off and relax is a problem.

Yet we cannot switch off from parenting, and that is the same problem. It is that mental overload of not ever being able to say, 'I am done for now. I do not want to think about that for a while'.

I know that the concept of being a 'full-time mum' is uncomfortable for some people because, of course, whether you are in paid work or not, you are a full-time mum or a full-time parent. The parenting doesn't stop, it's just that the other work comes and goes throughout the day. The reality is that parenting is a job and some parents have that as their single job, and other parents work additional jobs, such as their paid jobs.

As we discussed in the last chapter, everyone has a huge number of obligations in their lives regardless of whether they have paid work. The point is that if you are parenting and you never switch off from it, no matter how many other obligations you have, all parents have that same mental load. They are never able to switch off. This is an issue, and taking a break from parenting is absolutely vital for our sanity. For our mental health and our enjoyment of life, and for our ability to be decent parents. I often say to people that a holiday with the kids is not a holiday. I do not mean a holiday with the kids is something awful – I have had many lovely holidays with my boys – but a holiday with the kids is a holiday from all of your other jobs and obligations; however, it is not a holiday from the parenting job. So if we are talking about taking a break and having an actual holiday, a break from work, that would be also a break from parenting ... being able to completely switch off.

What that requires, when you are a parent, is being phys-ically away from the children. If someone else in the house offers to look after the kids but you can still hear them, you still have the mental load. You need them to be with someone who you know can handle it so you can be away. Obviously, we would always want our children to be with someone who will care for them well, but in order for us to have a break we also need them to be with someone who can handle things without running to you or texting you to check things every five minutes. We need to be able to switch off.

The Covid-19 pandemic, which is still ongoing at time of writing, has meant that at times of lockdown we really have been at work as parents 24/7, during lockdowns or if your children were isolating. People working from home due to the pandemic, for whom working from home is a new experience, found that it was even harder to switch off from work when work and home were the same place, and, of course as parents, having the children around so much, we have had even less opportunity to take a breather when they are with somebody else, such as school or childcare.

If you were working every waking hour and sleeping in the office, with no break, people would understand that was a problem! They would understand you are most likely overwhelmed ... they would be concerned! Yet unfortunately, we do not give the same consideration to ourselves and others when it comes to parenting.

Mindset Block Alert!

If I do not enjoy parenting all of the time, I am not a good parent, I am not doing it well enough.

If we look at what parenting actually involves, how on earth would we enjoy every moment of that experience? It is just not possible. Just as not enjoying everything about your job does not make you a bad employee, not enjoying everything about parenting does not say anything about your parenting – it just tells us you are a sane human being!

As parents we are, of course, all self-employed in that role. We have chosen it and the great thing about that is it means we can choose what our success criteria are and what our goals are. Not only do we not have to enjoy every single second of it, or in fact we do not have to enjoy any of it that isn't enjoyable, but we can also choose what success looks like to us. So often that is something that we unconsciously allow society to impose upon us: what it means to be a good parent. If I had been going to write this chapter as the guide to good parenting, how to do it well, the first question you should have been asking me is, 'Hang on a moment, who is to say that my aims are your aims?' I might have a completely different measure of success in parenting from you. It is so easy to be judgemental and say that someone is not doing a great job or is not a brilliant parent, but whilst that may be true by your measures, and, of course, there are legal basics to which we all have to adhere in parenting, it might be that the parent you are judging has a completely different set of aims from you.

You can decide what it means to be a good parent to your children. Moreover, remember that no matter what we decide and no matter what we are aiming for, we are not actually in control of the outcome anyway. The children have agency over their own lives, so we only have so much control in any case. At least we can remember, though, that we do not have to buy into anybody else's success criteria.

We do not have to enjoy anything about parenting that is not enjoyable, and we do not have to follow anybody else's rules for what it looks like to do it well.

How to make it more enjoyable is entirely up to you. If you look at it clearly and you find that there is a huge amount of parenting that you do not enjoy, you have the choice to do things differently. You have all of the decisions to make, and the only thing holding you back from making those decisions is what you imagine other people will think. In reality other people are mainly busy being concerned with what they are doing. The one thing we can say for sure, for anybody doing any kind of parenting, is that it is full on, relentless and no joke. Also, of course, hugely rewarding, otherwise nobody would do it, but let's be real about it. Let's not pretend that it is some kind of constantly happy and joyous experience. Let's be real about what it takes out of us and what we, therefore, need to put back into ourselves in order to do it well.

When we do need a break (and we all need a break) and taking a break is the sensible choice, we often need to get creative with how that can be achieved. Not everybody is fortunate enough to have people who can look after their children, and not everyone is fortunate enough to be able to afford people who can look after their children. So, I am not suggesting that it is easy to take a break, even if you get over the mindset block of doing it – there are practical issues as well. Often, though, there is a creative way around it, and it usually involves asking somebody to help, being willing to admit we need help, and being content in the fact that it is normal. All parents need to take a break from that job, in the same way that all employees need to take a break from their paid work.

It is useful to think about parenting as a job, and when I think of it that way it helps me to understand what I need and what can be reasonably expected of me. I do not expect day-to-day tremendous joy from every second. I do expect it to be a massively rewarding experience that will eventually give me back everything that I put into it, but I know it is going to take a lot out of me in the first instance. We all need to be mindful of that when we are trying to figure out how to get the most out of our lives and how our children can get the most out of their lives.

Thinking Points

- ♀ Parenting is a job and it has many of the same characteristics as paid employment.
- ♀ Not taking a break from the mental load of parenting is just as detrimental as not taking a break from the mental load of paid work.
- ♀ It makes no sense to imagine that we will enjoy every moment, or even the majority, of parenting when we consider what is involved in the job.
- ♀ How can you make parenting more enjoyable for *you*? What are *your* measures for good parenting, as opposed to the rules of outsiders which are not really serving you?

SEX

Yep, we are going there. If there is one subject around which there is an enormous amount of bullshit, it is sex. Especially where women are concerned, although I suspect men have their own sets of nonsense around the subject. We all have our hang-ups, we all have our concerns and worries, and we all need it and hopefully enjoy it.

So, let's dive straight in. The first thing I want to talk about is this: who you are with if you are in a sexual partnership, and what you are thinking about in order to turn yourself on and reach orgasm are, most of the time, two different things. Let us dispel that myth first, because I know that growing up I thought that the process was that you fancied someone, thought they were attractive, thought you would like to have sex with them, and then you had sex with them and the mere fact that they were naked in your bed and doing amazing things to your body (although admittedly in my youth the things they were doing weren't that amazing) would mean that the earth would move and it would be the most incredible experience. Their mere presence would do the job.

I hate to break it to any of you reading this who are not

yet aware of this, but our mere presence is very rarely enough to do the job for anybody. Most people have fantasies, kinks, triggers, whatever you want to call them, the things they think about when they are on their own in order to reach orgasm, and those are the things that work for them. Recognising that this is totally normal and necessary and is not a problem, it is how it is, is important.

When we were younger and we were reading the teen or adult magazines that were too old for us, we often saw articles about *Ten Tips To A Great Sex Life*, and somewhere in there would be a tip about telling your partner what it is that you like. For a start, I used to think at that point that I would rather poke my eyes out with a stick than discuss with anybody what I liked sexually, but I also thought that meant what I liked physically. Blow in my ears, kiss my neck, tickle my knees, whatever it is that you are into! I thought that is what it meant when we were encouraged to tell our partner what we like, and, of course, it does to a certain extent, especially if you have something specific that you really enjoy. Actually, though, I have come to realise that what it really means is talking about what is in our heads. Which, of course, is enormously daunting if you have never done it before, and you are not sure that the person you are with is on the same page as you.

My experience has been that people are usually way more on the same page as me than I imagined they would be, everything I have ever mumbled or quietly suggested has been greeted with great enthusiasm. It is so worth it. With your partner, tell them what is in your head and ask them to tell you what is in theirs. Instead of both of you being in your own heads, and pretending that is not the case, how about helping each other with those thoughts?

Do not panic, this does not have to lead to some appallingly cheesy role-play scenario if your partner says they like to think about this, that and the other and you imagine those thoughts are something you have to act out. Feel free, go as far with it as you like, but you do not have to reveal a kink or fantasy and then immediately buy the costume and make the home movie. Sometimes just talking about it, in the moment or at other times, is exciting enough. Once you know a thought or fantasy that your partner enjoys, you can find a picture of that or something that you know they will like connected to that thought, and just sharing that with them can be so intimate. Helping somebody else with their fantasies and being a part of it is wonderful. Not only are you the person they want to be with physically, but you also become the person they want to be with mentally.

Texting can be amazing if you are a little nervous, which we all are, about sharing your sexual thoughts. I generally find that sending a text is the first step: I can say things in writing that I would find excruciating to say verbally. Sending text messages, testing out ideas, gives your partner a chance to respond to new concepts in the way they would want to. If your partner turns to you and suddenly reveals they have a long-standing fantasy, you may respond in an unhelpful way in the moment. Yet if they send you a text message, it gives you the chance to have your initial reaction, think it through and then respond with something helpful and encouraging. It can be a good way to ease everyone into the discussion.

Fantasies are meaningful, but they often do not mean what is revealed on the surface. There are generally themes to fantasies, for example need, vulnerability, dominance, power, urgency, validation, comfort, the idea of having no responsibility or need to think things through, these are often themes that can create fantasies about things that might be a bad idea in real life. Our fantasies might be about things that could cause problems in real life or about things that you would never actually wish to do. Yet these are the themes that tend to work for us, and our mind will take us to where it wants us to go with them. Do not feel as though a thought you really liked means that you are going to act out that thought in real life. All it means is that there is a theme that works well for you and in the privacy of your own head or in the intimacy of discussions with your partner you can explore that.

All you ever need to do is what you are comfortable with.

I have done amateur porn in my time. I have recorded audios for an online social media forum. I came across a brilliant community, really enjoyed what they were doing and wanted to join in because I am the kind of person who dives in feet first! I have been a part of that amazing community and, therefore, I have a real fondness for porn done well, and done by amateurs. Exploitation and money-making in porn is a discussion for another day, but if you have amateurs making content for their own and each others' pleasure, no money changing hands, I have found it is one of the most supportive kinds of community. It is realism. Nothing fake. You get what people really sound like when they are turned on. What they really think about. How long people really take to reach orgasm – that is important information! Women typically take around twenty minutes to reach orgasm from the first point at which they are stimulated – sometimes guys do too! Sometimes we don't, and sometimes they don't!

There is a huge amount of acceptance in the amateur porn community, and it turns out that we all have similar kinks. The things you are thinking about that you feel you could never admit to, it turns out loads of people like that too, they think about it too, hell! there are websites dedicated to it. Whatever it is. You are not alone. It has all been done before, thought about before, supported and accepted before. It is all part of a fantastic experience, which is exploring what our bodies and minds enjoy.

It is such a vital part of life, it really is crazy that we do not discuss sex more than we do. How can we be happy, contended, productive, calm and confident members of society if we are not having our sexual needs met? Those needs are so important, but we discuss anything and everything else and sex is an afterthought. Yet it is one of our most basic needs.

Television, film, the media would have us believe that sex is all soft lighting and missionary position sex. Unless they want to point out that a female character is feeling particularly empowered, then she might be on top. Racy right? Or some guy is exerting his power, in which case he is going to bend the female character over and take her from behind. In the world of the media, no woman enjoys being bent over for sex, it is not a normal sexual position. Crazy, yes? Sexual positions do not actually have the meanings the media would ascribe to them, everyone simply has different ways that their bodies respond and, therefore, different positions that they enjoy. You can do what you want; there is no correct way to do it and no 'type' of person who does certain things.

There is not actually a 'type' of person who likes to be tied to the bedposts, or wear revealing lingerie or use sex toys. Lots of different people do those things, and lots of people do not. If you have ever looked at things in sex shops or on websites and thought *If I buy that does it mean I suddenly have to have a 1980s hairstyle and be screaming or breathless?* the answer is no! You just have to be you and see what works for you. Just do you! You do not have to become a different character to enjoy all of the rich variety that there is out there to enhance your sex life. You can do it the way that you want to do it.

What you want to do, as a woman, will change over the course of the month. We talked previously about our monthly cycle in terms of our energy levels and creativity – our sex drive also changes over the course of the month, as do our fantasies and desires and what works for us physically. That all changes week on week. It is a good idea to be open about that too. Yes, last week you really wanted this, but this week your hormones are in a different place so sex this week needs to have a different focus and a different approach. It can be difficult to discuss this stuff with your partner if you have not before, but it is enormously helpful. It can be wonderful to discuss it with the person you are with because then you both discover how to really blow each other's minds and then it is all pretty amazing and well worth the trouble.

Your sexual satisfaction is your right and also your responsibility. The idea that some handsome dude is going to ride into town and suddenly awaken all of your deepest desires is erroneous. You need to already know what they are and awaken them yourself, and then if the dreamboat turns up as well, that's great! Either way, you take responsibility for enjoying what you need to enjoy.

Thinking Points

- ♀ Who you are with, if you are in a sexual partnership, and what you are thinking about in order to turn yourself on and reach orgasm are, most of the time, two different things.
- ♀ Helping somebody else with their fantasies and being a part of it is wonderful.
- ♀ Fantasies are the mind's free exploration of certain key themes – they never need to be explored in reality if that is not practical, not legal or simply not comfortable.
- ♀ Whatever is in your fantasies, you are not alone. It has all been done before, thought about before, supported and accepted before.
- ♀ Sex is one of our most basic needs. There is no correct way to do it and no 'type' of person who does certain things.
- ♀ As a woman, your needs, fantasies and desires will change with your menstrual cycle.

RELATIONSHIPS

This chapter focuses on our intimate, romantic relationships, but a lot of what is discussed will also hold true for our other relationships. I am a divorced woman, so you may have some idea of some of the things I am going to say! I do not feel that marriage is a sham or a bad idea. I am not going to tell you not to do it or to get out of it. I do, however, feel strongly that there is a societal narrative about the way that life should look, which is get married, have children, stay together forever. I have no problem with that story, I have no problem with a hundred other stories, what I am keen to do is ensure that you know that you can choose your own story. There are no 'shoulds', just lots of value judgements and opinions from other people. We can write our own story and that is very important.

How do our relationships fit in with the story that we want to be living?

I often coach women who are in their late thirties or early forties; they are in a relationship and there some problems because every relationship comes with its ups and downs. They are often searching for reassurance that it is not all their fault and, also, a way they can make it all work. Maybe a while ago they gave up on trying to get the other person to help to make it work, and they are stuck in this feeling that this is their life and they have to make it work, somehow.

 ## *Mindset Block Alert!*

It is not possible for me to change anything about my relationship, or to change the relationship I am in,

You can change things, now or in the future. The idea that you are stuck with something and you have to make the best of it – that is a choice, but it is not the only choice.

Changing things does not necessarily mean breaking up the relationship. That is one of the choices, but the important thing to do is look your relationship full in the face. You may decide that this is it, you want to be in this relationship no matter what. You may decide that you want things to change within the relationship, and you are going to do your best to keep the relationship together but something has to change. Ending the relationship is another choice. Those choices are always on the table. They each have pros and cons, things to figure out, things that may worry you or excite you or frighten you. When we close the door on those choices before fully exploring them we do ourselves a disservice.

Most of us have got to where we are in our relationships because of choices a much younger person made. Perhaps that person was not fully realised, perhaps they wanted different things, they are not the person that you are now. On the basis that change can happen at any time and in many ways, rather than looking at where you are now, let's get a blank piece of paper and figure out, from the point of view of the person you are today, how you want to feel in your life, day to day. How do you want to feel every day or most days? On a good day, how do you want life to feel to you? What do you want a relationship for? What is really important to you? Relationships can give us all kinds of different things, and I cannot tell you what should be your priorities. What does a relationship give to you that you would not have if you were single? How do you want it to add value to your life?

When I talk about a relationship adding value that is because I feel very strongly that our most important relationship is the one we have with ourselves. Many of us do not give ourselves enough of a chance to build that relationship. Rather than ending up in a place where we have cobbled together a bit of emotional safety, a bit of intimacy, some practical help around the house and some financial support and feel as though that is life, what would it be like if we thought about ourselves as whole fulfilled people? With the potential to do almost everything we need for ourselves?

We might not be financially independent because we have chosen not to be in paid work for any number of reasons. This is all about looking at your circumstances full in the face. Yet if we could be financially independent, build up our practical skills if we don't have those, and give ourselves a good amount of emotional safety, managing our own minds and emotions pretty effectively, if we could give ourselves all of those things, what would we then want in a relationship? That is what I mean by adding value: what is it we want a relationship to bring to our already whole lives?

It is a very different thought process to imagining we need things from other people and could not cope on our own. It is important to look at that blank piece of paper, who you are now and what you would want from someone else in your life, because that is going to help you to understand what it is you need from your relationships now, be it the relationship you are already in or a new one that you are looking for.

We all have our own view on what a relationship is for and what it should look like, and I am not here to say that I have the definitive answer to that. I do have *an* answer to that though, and I will outline it to you to see if it is helpful to you. To me, a good relationship helps us to be the best version of ourselves that we can be. It helps us to grow and to reach our goals. It helps us to feel fulfilled and it builds us up. Of course, in a good relationship those things cut both ways, so the person I am with feels as though I help them to be the best version of themselves, I help them to grow and reach their goals and feel fulfilled, and I build them up. To me, that is the value a relationship adds. To have the feeling someone gives you that, and you are giving that to someone else, is incredible.

When we are approaching or at middle age, we may have children in the mix and we have a lot going on, so often our relationship has become simply another pair of hands or another pay cheque. We could potentially find that practical help or financial input somewhere else, and it is about looking that full in the face. I am not suggesting you kick out your partner today, get a job and pay your own bills. I am suggest-ing that it would be helpful to be honest with yourself if the main reason you are in this relationship is because you need the financial support and it is good to have someone who knows how to change a tyre or fix the boiler. You have not done something dreadfully wrong if that is the case, it is not an unusual situation to be in, but let's look at it honestly. Then we can know what choices we are making.

Is the story that you want to tell for the rest of your life that you chose to be in a relationship mainly for practical support, and perhaps you therefore sacrificed other things that a rela-tionship could bring? If you are happy with that story, if that is the story you want to choose, there is nothing wrong with that. I do, however, urge us all to know what story we are choosing and not to be blind to it. When we choose our story, with eyes wide open, that is the way to avoid regret. When we choose our path and see it for what it is. Regrets and resentment build up when we bury the reality of our situation.

We only have one life, as far as I know. We get to a certain point at what feels like mid-way through life where we have to choose how it is going to play out, and what it is that we actually want. As women, statistically speaking, no matter who we choose or what we pick, we are probably going to end up in an old folks' home surrounded by other women. We tend to outlive the guys. On that basis, if we are all going to end up sitting together looking back on our lives, no matter who or what we chose, I personally want to be able to look back with a sense of satisfaction in my choices. I do not want to look back with regret.

There is nothing wrong with devoting your whole life to a romantic partner, to your children, to anything at all. What I would say is a problem, though, is when we do not devote our lives to ourselves first. You are the centre of your circle, you are the central point. After that, it is a question of who are you inviting in? If we have children, they have to be invited in, we are responsible for them. Everybody else is optional. Everybody else. You have no obligation to invite anybody else into your circle. Who are you inviting in? Rather than keeping the door open the whole time, who is it that you are inviting into your 'one wild and precious life' as the late Mary Oliver terms it?

If you find that you are not telling the story you want to tell, and you have invited in people who you no longer want in your space, or you do not know how to invite in the people you do want in your space, it is time to make some changes. Potentially with support.

A truly fulfilling relationship is an incredible thing, and I do not want you to miss out on that.

Thinking Points

- 💡 How does your relationship fit in with the story you want to be living?
- 💡 You always have the choice to make changes in a relationship.
- 💡 How do you want a relationship to add value to your life?

💡 A good relationship helps us to be the best version of ourselves that we can be. It helps us to grow and to reach our goals. It helps us to feel fulfilled and it builds us up.

💡 Regrets and resentment build up when we bury the reality of our situation.

💡 Are you inviting the right people into your life?

LIFE GOALS

Having covered some business essentials, a lot of ideas about self-worth and then having had a look at our non-work life and relationships, what exactly are we doing it all for? Do you have a clear picture of where you are headed? Does the concept of having life goals sound exciting or intimidating? Do not worry, I am not going to suggest that you must have enormous life goals that stretch and challenge you, that is not what I am about.

Any goals, but particularly big life goals, come with the caveat that we do not know what the future holds. Sometimes, it can feel as though there is very little point setting big goals, and I understand that feeling. If we look back over the last ten years at everything that has happened globally and everything that has happened to us personally, most of it we could not have predicted. Some of it has been far better than we expected, some of it has completely thrown our plans out of the window, and a lot of it has been challenging, but most of it has certainly been unpredictable. So I understand when people say that there is not much point making a plan.

I have to admit, I do not have much of a plan, partly

because I am unmarried, so I can roll with the changes and the punches, I do not have somebody else's life plan running alongside mine. It is also because over the last ten years of my life and my family's life there has been such immense change and growth and learning it seems a little less exciting to me now to have a big plan, as I am curious to see what just happens! However, there is one thing that I do think it is worth thinking about and that is how we want to feel.

I do not ask my children what they want to be when they grow up: I ask them how they want to feel in their adult life. Partly because that would have been a useful question for someone to have asked me when I was younger. Most of the things that I want in life are based on how I think they will make me feel and how I would like to feel. How we want to feel can focus our mind in a different way. If we have reached a certain point in our lives or a certain point in our career, setting new goals can feel like a box-ticking exercise. There might be big exciting things that we want to do, or we might be content with what we are doing and not need a large detailed plan for world domination. It could still, though, be important to think about how we want to feel, especially if we are currently feeling overwhelmed, lacking in confidence or lacking in self-belief, if we imagine there are things we cannot do because of who we are. So thinking about how we want to feel could be the most important goal to consider.

As I have asked before, what do you want more of and what do you want less of? Feelings, objects, opportunities, anything? What balance needs to change to help you to feel how you would like to feel?

If you have a partner in your life who has a stake in your future and you have a stake in theirs, another question to ask is how do you picture your future? If I imagine myself in old age, I picture myself in a care home. I have worked in a care home, my grandparents and great-grandparents were in care homes; growing up, it was normal to me that that is where you live when you are an elderly person. Those pictures we have in our heads are important because at some point it will be useful for the people in my life to know that is what I picture and what I am comfortable with. If we do not share that information, there is no way other people can know. You may have an image in your head of what retirement looks like or what being a certain age looks like, what it looks like when the kids leave home or when you sell your business. Share those visions, because the person you are with may have a completely different picture in their heads. That is no reason to panic, but it is a reason to have a good chat and figure out how to bring those pictures together, or why you have those visions in the first place and what are the important elements of them?

Make sure you are both picturing a future that excites you.

Some people say that you should not set goals because if it 'goes wrong' it leads to disappointment. That is a misunderstanding of what plans or goals are about. If I set myself a goal and something changes that is outside my control which makes that goal impossible, that does not mean it was a pointless goal. There will be things about that goal upon which I can still focus, there will still be important elements of it that I need to have in my life. Those feelings and experiences could still be achievable in a different way, if they are still important to me.

Goals are not boxes to tick regardless of how we feel, they are things that we really want. They are markers for the journey of our lives. We are all journeying through our lives and we can't see very far ahead. When we have certain goals, those give us a destination point so when we come across choices to make or decisions to take, those things are easier to navigate because we know where we are headed and what our priorities are. It helps us to spot the opportunities that are relevant to us and to take the right ones when they are presented to us.

As we go down the roads of life's journey, some paths will be blocked, some will be challenging and there will be times when we decide to change the destination. This is not about success or failure, it is about mapping out our journey. If we decide to change the destination, that simply means that we are going to start taking different paths and making different choices. It is all forward motion. We cannot help but move forward through our lives – we cannot time travel backwards! We might feel that it is not at all useful to us to have any destination in mind at all, but it can be helpful so we know which turn to take next.

Mindset Block Alert!

When setting goals I often come up with something amazing and then talk myself out of it by coming up with all of the challenges.

When you are thinking about goals, do not try to think about the whys and hows and wherefores before you have fully focused on the goals. So often, we talk ourselves out of a goal because we think it is out of our reach. Yet we are going to think most things are out of our reach if we are not doing them right now. The reality is that if there is something you want, there will be multiple ways to achieve that or to start working towards it. Have it as a goal and let it sit for a bit. Just let it settle in your mind, and then you get creative with opportunities and options for making it happen. Or simply just let it sit there in your mind even if you have no idea how you are going to achieve it, because once it is fixed in your mind you will start to spot the opportunities that exist around you to get you closer to it, even if, to begin with, you cannot imagine what those might be.

Do not give up on a dream because of the time it will take.
That time will pass anyway.

(Earl Nightingale)

If you come up with a goal, you are creative about ways in which you can achieve it; you see all the opportunities to get started with it and you still know that it is going to take, say, five years to achieve it – those five years will pass anyway. If you are lucky. So you can either be five years on not having done anything to reach that goal, or five years on having achieved it. The time will pass anyway, the question is how do you want to feel and how do you want to pass that time? How can you get creative in figuring out how to get there?

Thinking Points

- 💡 What do you want more of and what do you want less of?
- 💡 What balance needs to change to help you to feel how you would like to feel?
- 💡 If you have a life partner, make sure you are both picturing a future that excites you.
- 💡 *Do not give up on a dream because of the time it will take. That time will pass anyway.*

A TALE OF FIVE WOMEN

I told this story to a friend the other day who encouraged me to turn it into a blog post, and I am inserting it here as I think it is relevant after a chapter about life goals. This story is about five women whom I met when I was working at a residential home for the elderly in my student days.

I worked in the kitchens and as a cleaner at the home. As it was a residential rather than a nursing home, most of the residents had dementia or simply needed a little assistance with their day-to-day lives. I met some wonderful people there – staff and residents – and learned an awful lot. Five women in particular, though, stand out in my memory.

I don't know whether there has been any research done on this, but my anecdotal evidence suggests that when somebody has dementia, it is their innermost values and needs that come to the fore as their inhibitions diminish. It really made me think about who I would be without social constraints and mental filters, and what would be my uppermost concerns. Four of the women at the home had very specific concerns. I have changed their names here but let me introduce you to Kitty, Florence, Marjorie, Ada and Annie.

Kitty's main concern was her little girl. She would ask every day where her little girl was; she was very concerned to make sure that she was okay. Her little girl was in fact now her adult daughter, but Kitty couldn't remember that. Her mind was firmly in 'mum' mode and she wanted to know her daughter's whereabouts. Fortunately, she was easy to reassure and did not become distressed as long as she was told her daughter was safe.

Florence was also very concerned with the whereabouts of something, but for Florence it was her money. She was very anxious about where her money was, to the point where a wallet with a few coins in was kept in her room because she would become distressed without it. She wasn't interested in how much there was, and certainly never suggested anything on which she wanted to spend it. She just needed to know that she had it.

Marjorie was horny. No question about it. There were very few men in the home, as is usually the case, but every week a middle-aged man would come in to give the residents some art therapy. Marjorie was always extremely happy to see him, and her face would light up whenever there was a man around. Beside her bed she had a lovely photograph of her wedding, and although it was bittersweet to see it, I liked to think that her enthusiasm for male company suggested that her romantic life had been a happy one.

Ada on the other hand was angry. Not all the time, a lot of the time she was fine, but she had a temper on her. Being trapped inside a mind with dementia must be incredibly frustrating, and Ada would display that at times. She still had her red hair so I guess, to use a stereotype, she was a fiery redhead. She rarely appeared anxious, but annoyed at the world in general? Oh yes.

Finally, we have Annie. Annie did not suffer from dementia; she was in the home because she was blind. Whilst I worked there, Annie celebrated her 100th birthday and got her telegram from the Queen.

Annie would sit calmly in her armchair every day, listening to the comings and goings, and was always happy to have a chat. Her favourite thing was to have someone read out the crossword clues to her so that she could do the crossword. She was a friendly woman who was always good company, and despite the fact that she was now in a home with a number of residents in various stages of dementia, she was always composed and seemed content. Two things I know about Annie: she never married, and she travelled extensively. She had had a fascinating life and had done all manner of things in her 100 years.

As women, if we are fortunate enough to live to a grand old age, the chances are we will find ourselves in a care home or residential setting of some kind with a lot of other women. Regardless of the romantic choices we make, that is probably where we will be. For my part, I hope that by then I have found all of my calm and have let go of the daily anxieties and nagging worries. I certainly do not want to become a prisoner to them if my mind loses its ability to manage itself effectively.

My aim has always been to squeeze every last drop of enjoyment out of life, and I think that is, in part, down to Annie. Knowing that she had been everywhere and done it all meant that she could face old age with equanimity and a whole host of memories.

Let's not end our days with frustrations, anxieties and regrets. Let's end our days with good memories, content in the knowledge that we left it all out on the field. With perhaps a dash of Marjorie's continued joie de vivre.

LIFE'S TOOLKIT

I will start with what this is not: this is not a chapter about good habits and consistency. This is a chapter about using the appropriate tools on the appropriate days.

I know that a lot of people will try to drum into you the idea that being consistent with good habits will change your life and help you reach your goals. That may well be true for some, but I believe that consistency is extremely difficult for most people to achieve. There are elements of consistency that are useful, but trying to do the same thing every day or even every week is really challenging, particularly if you are person who has a monthly hormonal cycle. If that is you, then your energy levels, confidence, self-belief, what you want and how you feel all change cyclically every four weeks in a fairly predictable pattern that makes consistency something of a futile aim. It is counterproductive to push ourselves past what is reasonable.

I have an approach that is a little different: I think about our tools. We have a big toolkit, and the older we get the more we put into it. The important thing is knowing when and how to use the tools that we have.

We have already talked about meeting our needs, under-standing and knowing what those needs are, and the things that we do to meet our needs are definitely part of the toolkit. For me, coffee, hot showers, comfy clothes, walks in the sun-shine and nice drives with my tunes on are all things I do to meet my needs and they are all tools in my toolkit. These are the first set of tools to be aware of: the things that you need in order to feel good, the things that make your day easier, the things that make your day more pleasant and that make you more productive.

Yet we cannot do everything all at once. We might be think-ing that we need to eat healthily and we need to exercise and get a handle on our finances and meditate and to have a better idea of our personal clothing style and get a grip on our busi-ness branding ... on and on it goes. We cannot do everything every day. We have to decide which tools are relevant for that day. Which tool do you need today? There will be some days when your body tells you that the most important tool you can access that day is some healthy food. There are going to be other days when what you really need to get a grip on is your budget and you are going to feel like eating cake while you do that, and that is okay.

Saying yes to one thing always means saying no to some-thing else, that is part of life. If you are training for a marathon you are saying yes to exercise and probably no to having a lie-in at the weekend. If that lie-in is an important tool for you to help you to feel good and be productive, you need to be aware that you are saying no to it for the whole time that you are saying yes to your training schedule. How is that going to feel, which other tools can you use to replace it or to mitigate the loss of it? It is about being savvy with what tools you are using, rather than expecting your body and mind to just perform however you want them to without any of the tools or input that they need.

We can say yes to the comfort that a nice hearty meal brings and accept on that day we are saying no to counting calories. It is not a good or a bad thing, it is just about understanding what we are saying yes or no to because of the tools we need that day.

The ultimate goal is that we keep functioning so that we can reach the goals we discussed in the previous chapter, the things that we want out of life. If we stop functioning well, we are not going to get anywhere. The goal when we think about our toolbox is to keep our bodies and minds running the way that we need them to so that we can do the things we want to do.

We have covered a huge amount so far in this book, and we need our tools in order to do any of it well. We also need to avoid beating ourselves up for not using all of our tools all of the time or for not using them consistently. Doing everything every day is just not possible.

When we bring new tools into the toolkit, sometimes we can think of these as fads or the latest craze. Actually, it is totally fine to try something new for just a short amount of time because we need lots of tools. If you spent three years doing Zumba and then you gave it up, and then later on you started to do Pilates, there is no reason to feel like you failed at being consistent with Zumba simply because you are not doing it for the rest of your life. It was a useful tool at the time, you will be able to tell me what it gave you, and now you are using a different tool. Zumba is always in your toolbox, and there may come a day when what it gave to you is what you need again, so you will go back to it. It is fine to be a bit 'faddy'. If your goal is to get strong, get healthy, get fit, move your body and do something active it doesn't matter if you do martial arts one year, tennis the next year and hockey the next. You are still achieving your goal and they are all useful tools.

Mindset Block Alert!

I do not value myself enough to use all of my tools.

What sometimes holds us back from using our tools is this feeling that we have somehow failed if we do not use them every day. When we think about some of our tools they bring up feelings of guilt because we stopped doing them consistently so now they are unpleasant to consider. Those feelings are just a story though; in reality, every time you use a tool, however sporadically, it gives you something that you need, and you can use that tool any time you want. You just need to value yourself enough to give yourself what you need when you need it.

We can know that a good walk in the sunshine or a good meditation session or a massage is going to make us feel so much better, but these things all take up time, and saying yes to one thing means saying no to another, so saying yes to having a massage one evening might mean saying no to putting your kids to bed; someone else may need to do that instead. That is okay. It is okay to say yes to using your tools and filling your cup and fulfilling your needs. Saying yes to anything that helps us to stay functioning and reaching our goals is beneficial to everyone around us, especially if we have had those conversations we talked about in the previous chapter, making sure that the people in our lives are on the same page with the goals we have.

It can be a real blockage to using our tools when we feel that we are not worth that time or that energy or input or that we are an inconvenience to other people. We have to value ourselves enough to make those suggestions and to come up with the creative solutions to get those things done. It is also important to understand what the tools are in the toolboxes of the people around us. There will be some things that the people in our lives do which annoy us or are confusing to us or we don't understand why they do them, but it might turn out that those things are some of their tools, and they need to use them and they need our support in using them. Have that conversation with the people around you, what are their tools? How do they fill their cup? How can you structure your days, weekends, lives, months, years so you all get to use your tools when you need them?

Do not be afraid to have a lot of tools and to try new things. Say yes to using your tools, understand which tools you are saying no to or which needs you are not fulfilling when you say yes to other things. It is all about awareness of how we are looking after ourselves and how we are expecting our bodies and minds to function, and the ways in which we can encourage them to function at their best. Forgive yourself for having a short attention span for some tools or for being inconsistent. The only thing that is a problem is when we do not use the tools that we know we need because we do not feel that we are worthy of that time or investment.

Thinking Points

- It is not about consistency, it is about using the appropriate tools at the appropriate times.
- Make a list of everything that you have in your toolkit.
- Each day, think about which tools will meet your needs.
- The goal is to keep our bodies and minds running the way that we need them to so that we can do the things we want to do.
- Value yourself enough to give yourself what you need when you need it.

RECOGNITION OF HOW FAR WE HAVE COME

We have done a fair amount of looking forward, but how about a little looking back? It can be difficult to reflect on our achievements and how far we have already come in life, partly because we might struggle to celebrate ourselves, partly because we imagine that somewhere out there is a perfect version of us that we are striving towards. As long as we are not that perfect version of ourselves (which we never actually can be) we keep pushing towards that perfect us, and we do not take time to look back and celebrate our progress because we imagine we are not done yet.

In reality, we start life with a personality, the person we are on the day that we are born, and with our circumstances. That is what we are born with. After that, it is all challenges and choices: that's life. There is actually no perfect to get to – that is never going to happen. We are never going to wake up or sit down in a chair with a cup of tea and think, *This is it. I've done it. Here I am, perfect.* It will be challenges and choices and wonderful things, that is life.

The things to look back on, whenever we want to, anytime we want to look back and reflect, are what we know now that we didn't know before. What skills have we developed? What have we learned? What strengths have we acquired? What challenges have we overcome, right from birth? What have we contributed, in any way that is meaningful to us? What do we have now that we did not have before? Whom have we loved, and who loves us?

It is really worth doing this, it is almost mindful to take that pause to recognise that there is a stream of life behind us as well as the present moment and the future we are anticipating.

It can be easy at this point to start making comparisons to what we think other people might say in answer to these questions. Yet the only comparison should be between yourself and your past self, that is the only meaningful comparison. Other people were born with different personalities and different circumstances, so comparing ourselves to them means nothing.

Why are we looking back? Partly to celebrate, as there is great value in celebrating our wins, our achievements and what we have overcome. Also, though, it is to remind yourself of what you can do. It sends those messages to your brain that you can face adversity or learn something new. You are able to overcome difficult feelings in order to achieve a goal. You can do these things because you have done these things. Particularly if you are trying something new, look back and remind yourself of what you have already done before you put new goals in place; it will make it easier for you to have faith that you can do new things.

We are never going to reach a plateau of perfection. We all imagine it, when we book a holiday or when we think about a free weekend or a family Christmas, we imagine that plateau of perfection when everything is perfect. We get flashes of that; if we are lucky, we have had moments of that. Those times we have been sitting on the beach with a drink in our hand or we are surrounded by family at Christmas and we think everything is right with the world, but they are just moments. We are never going to reach a plateau of feeling that way for more than maybe thirty minutes, before someone has a row or the dishes need doing or we realise we are sunburned or some problem arises.

Our whole lives we are going to be climbing mountains, enjoying views and resting in valleys. That's the journey of life. We can choose when to climb and when to rest; we can choose to never climb a mountain again, but that is the journey. That is what is ahead of us and what is behind us, and each mountain in front of us is going to be much easier to climb or easier to face if we spend some time turning around and looking back at all of the mountains that we have already climbed. There are a lot of mountains behind us. I don't care how big yours are or what they were, they do not need to be compared to my mountains or to anyone else's. There are a lot of mountains and you climbed them all. You might have been swearing and crying the whole way, I know I was! We climbed them though, and we took in the view, and we rested in the valley, and we climbed a new one, through choice or because it was forced upon us.

Mindset Block Alert!

I compare myself to others and feel
I have to earn the right to reflect
and celebrate and feel proud.

It is so worth looking back and recognising that we did that so that when we look at the mountains ahead we can choose which ones to climb and we can have confidence that we can do it.

There will have been times when we did not get to the top of the mountain: we thought, *Sod this stupid mountain* and we went back down again and went round it. Or we fell off the mountain and made a mess of things. There will be times when we chose not to climb a really big mountain. That can all make us feel as though we do not deserve to reflect and celebrate because we imagine that other people have climbed all their big mountains and have had bigger challenges. In actual fact, you don't know anything about their journey and what they have chosen and what challenges they have had. Even if they have told you in great details, that is still only a story they have told. You were not there doing that climb, you do not know anything about it. There really is no point comparing, and we all deserve to look back and reflect on the challenges we have faced.

We started when we were born. With a long life behind you, you will have plenty on which to reflect, the same as everyone else does, and no matter what choices you have made you still deserve to be proud. It is important to be proud, and remind yourself of your capabilities. Your journey is your own. Others are going to view it as hard or easy, inspiring or uninteresting, and that does not matter. It is your journey, and how you see it is what counts.

If you do look back at your journey and you genuinely feel like you have not been on the right path, you are always capable of change. That is the other great thing about reflection, it allows us to gain that clarity. You do not have to climb the mountain in front of you if it is not really the one you want to climb. You can change the path at any time. Getting that clarity through reflection can help you to decide which path you would like to follow next.

Be sure to do some reflection before you make new plans. It is far easier to do something new when you take the time to remind yourself how far you have already come.

Thinking Points

- ♀ Life is all challenges and choices – there is no perfect to get to.
- ♀ What do you know now that you didn't know before? What skills have you developed? What have you learned? What strengths have you acquired? What challenges have you overcome, right from birth? What have you contributed, in any way that is meaningful to you? What do you have now that you did not have before? Whom have you loved, and who loves you?

- ♀ Look back to recognise what you have already overcome.
- ♀ Look back to get clarity on where you want to go next.
- ♀ Look back to celebrate everything you have already achieved.

BEING IN THE MOMENT

The future is ours to create. The past is ours to celebrate or perhaps reflect upon. What about the present?

Many of us struggle to be in the moment, not least because in most moments we are actually on our phones. The struggle is real! To dig into how we can be more present I am going to, yet again, go for an extended metaphor.

Let us start with the phrase 'sink or swim'. You will have heard that phrase. Are those the only two options in life? I think we all know what they both feel like. Sinking, or drowning as I think of it, are the times when it has all gone to shit. The black dog of depression is upon us, we are overwhelmed, anxiety is out of control. You will know what drowning feels like for you. Hopefully it is not happening all of the time, although for some people it will be.

Swimming is the other end of that scale. These are the times when we are making progress. Winning a new client, having a parenting breakthrough, figuring out an issue with which we have been struggling, clearing crap out of our houses … Again, it will look different for all of us. But we know when

we are swimming. When we are moving forward, making progress, feeling good.

The majority of life, though, does not involve sinking or
swimming. The drowning times are hopefully few and far
between, and really, so are the swimming times because we
cannot be making progress all the time. That would be crazy,
and it is not possible or, at least, it is not sustainable.

So what do we do for the rest of the time? The rest of
the moments in our day when we are just 'being'? The school
run, the grocery shop, the precious free time before bed, the
moments with our friends, all the other stuff? What are we
doing then?

I have decided that I have two choices in all of those
moments. I can tread water ... or I can float.

Treading water used to be my default: it is an easy habit to
slip into, and we all know when we are doing it. Treading water
means expending lots of energy just to stay still. Keeping
moving even though we are not going anywhere. Sometimes, it
is keeping moving in a desperate attempt to avoid the drowning – numbing ourselves, distracting ourselves because we
know that actually we are on the brink of burnout and we are
treading water in order to stop going under. Sometimes we
are treading water because we wish we were swimming or we
think we 'should' be swimming, so we keep moving; we do not
really know how to stop.

It is exhausting. It depletes our energy, making it harder
to then swim forward when we have the opportunity. We use
all this energy just to stay still, and because it is exhausting it

actually makes it more likely we will start to drown. We are not taking time to rest and be in the moment; it gets us nowhere, and it is so very tiring.

So instead of expending all this energy treading water, when we talk about being in the moment that is when we can choose instead to float.

Floating takes no energy, or very little. Floating is calm and slow and it allows us to breathe and to think. It builds up our reserves for the next time that we need to swim, whilst at the same time keeping us safe from drowning, almost indefinitely. It is a far healthier, far more productive choice. And it feels so lovely.

Yet a lot of us will struggle to float. Why? Because in order to float we need to stop. You cannot float and swim: that is treading water! You have to stop in order to float and in order to be in that moment, just being. Cessation of movement is difficult because we feel like we should be swimming ALL THE TIME, and if we stop moving we are admitting that we are not swimming. As long as we are treading water we are fooling ourselves and maybe others into thinking that we are still doing, even if we have nothing to do and we are scrolling through social media or cleaning something that is already clean. We do not want to admit that we have stopped and there is no swimming to be done right now.

Yet it is okay to stop. If we are not swimming, and thankfully we are not drowning, the best course of action is to float. Give yourself permission to stop treading water. It is depleting your energy reserves, and it is getting you nowhere.

What floating actually looks like, what it means to stop

and be in the moment, will differ from person to person. For some people it will be specific activities – you might be floating when you are doing yoga, or knitting, or walking outside, or meditating. Or spending time in an actual flotation tank. There are lots of activities which make it easier to float. It is easier to be mindful and in the moment when you are on a nice sunny walk rather than when you are on the school run or making the dinner. Yet I really have been trying, for me, to make it a moment-by-moment thing.

The challenge is to try to float no matter what we are doing. For me, it is a deep breath, an acknowledgement of my surroundings, a bit of grounding in the moment. Some people would call it mindfulness, whatever works for you. It is an understanding that I do not actually need to check Facebook, message my friend with my latest stream of consciousness, load the dishwasher straightaway, check my emails for another task, wander from room to room looking for activity … I am not swimming, I am not drowning. So I just float.

When I first came up with this concept I thought how useful it would have been when I had newborn babies. This is so relevant to new parents because parenting a baby is the ultimate in treading water. You can achieve nothing, or nothing that you recognise as an achievement at the time. You are constantly trying not to drown because you are exhausted, and your mental and physical health have taken a hammering. So you create pointless mindless activity because you miss swimming, and you don't know how to just stop. People told me at the time to 'go with the flow', but that meant nothing to me. I had no idea what that meant at that time in my life.

What I needed was to be shown how to float.

Of course, no new mother can actually take on board sensible advice at the time! It is all just too hard. When I thought at the time I was drowning, I was actually just desperately missing swimming, and learning to float would have helped me a lot.

So the next time you do not message me back straight away, or 'like' my Instagram post, or get my birthday card to me on time, or remember that thing I told you about a while back ... do not worry. I will not be offended. I will not be worried. I will know you have put aside what for you feels like pointless activity for a little while. If you are taking some time out, I will know you are floating. There will be times when I am floating. If we both do some of that, if we all do some of that, when we are ready and rested and re-energised we can get swimming together again and make the progress.

If you want to be in the moment and you are anything like me, the first thing to do is recognise that we need to give ourselves permission to stop, and we do not need to be constantly 'doing'. Not all activity is progressing things, some is activity for activity's sake because being active makes us feel as though we are doing the 'right' thing. Stopping makes us feel like we are doing the 'wrong' thing. Yet we have to retain and replenish our energy, otherwise we are going to drown. If we float, we can survive for much longer and be ready to swim when we can.

Thinking Points

- ♀ It is okay to stop.
- ♀ If we are not swimming, and thankfully we are not drowning, the best course of action is to float.
- ♀ Give yourself permission to stop treading water. It is depleting your energy reserves, and it is getting you nowhere.
- ♀ What does floating look like to you?

FEAR AND ANXIETY

Putting into practice any ideas about how to have a happier life can sound straightforward on a good day when we are feeling fantastic. Yet that is not every day, not by a long chalk. Logic and rational thinking is only one part of what is going on inside our brains. Another big part? Our fears and our anxieties.

As somebody who has medically diagnosed anxiety, as somebody who takes medication for anxiety and has done for some time, anxiety is not about what is happening in my life, it is just a fact that I have anxiety. With that said, even for those of us who do not have a mental health challenge, feeling anxious and overwhelmed is a completely normal part of running a business and is normal part of life. It happens.

We have all of these fantastic ideas, goals and dreams, places we want to get to, and then there is that little voice that says, *What if it all goes wrong?* We have the fear! We have the fear, and we have the anxiety.

I really like the phrase 'feel the fear and do it anyway' because of how I interpret it. Some people think it means forget the fact that you are scared and do it anyway, do not manage that fear or look after yourself, just do it anyway! That is not how I interpret that phrase at all.

I used to think there would be a time when I no longer had that little voice, that little, *What if it all goes wrong? What if everybody hates me? What if I get laughed at?* I thought that at some point I would no longer have any of those brain weasels; I would get to a stage where I felt confident and on top of everything all of the time. I know now that is not how it is going to be, not because I have anxiety, but because I am a human. My unconscious mind is always going to be scared of change, and it is always going to hate the vulnerability that comes with trying something new or putting myself out there. That is just how all of our unconscious minds work – they like safety and they like familiarity. They do not like change, and they do not like trying things.

Dr Brené Brown talks at length about the vulnerability of stepping into the arena, of saying, 'Here I am, and this is what I can do'. We can manage that feeling, but it is not going to go away. So what I have promised myself is this: I am never going to let fear hold me back. I am not going to look at my fears and think that they mean that I cannot do the thing I want to do. I might choose not to do things for many other reasons, but I am not going to make that choice through fear.

My solution, therefore, my interpretation of 'feel the fear and do it anyway' is to separate out the anxiety from the goals. My anxiety is this big bag that I am pulling along behind me, some days it is really heavy, other days it is not too bad, but I am going to walk forwards anyway. I have my big bag of anxiety and here I go, pulling it along. So how do we separate it out?

The important thing is to see it for what it is. We need to recognise what is not serving us. For instance, if you think to yourself, *I do not know very much about topic X, that is something I would like to know about, I am going to look into some training*, that is a sensible way to improve your skills. If, however, your thought process is, *I do not know as much about topic X as other people do, I should shut my mouth and never talk about it ever again*, that is unhelpful anxiety. We need to deal with that separately but not let it stop us from learning and growing and achieving.

How on earth do we do that? We put it aside. We book the training course, we sign up to the networking event, we say yes to the meeting, we agree to the phone call, whatever it is that is going to get us further towards our goals, we get it done. I know that is easy to say, but we get it done. We put our big bag of anxiety to one side; it can wait until later. That's the feel the fear and do it anyway part; we get it done because we know it is moving us further towards our goals and we have chosen those goals for a reason.

This is the crucial bit, though, that people often miss out: when it is done and you are on the path to wherever you want to be, then it is time to look after your unconscious mind. Then it is time to get yourself feeling safe. Your unconscious mind is now panicking, so now is the time for the hot drink and the warm blanket and the scented candle – feed your senses, give your mind and body every comfort they desire. Treat yourself with that excessive kindness, and do not be angry with yourself for having fear that is completely normal and understandable. It is human. Do whatever you need to do to make yourself feel better, and do not begrudge yourself that kindness. Go for a walk, have a luxurious bath, sing along to the loud music, whatever it takes to make yourself feel calm.

It is not about shying away from things because you are afraid, but neither is it about expecting yourself to 'get a grip' and squash down your rising anxiety. It is about putting the anxiety to one side, doing what needs to be done and then picking up the bag of anxiety and focusing on what your little anxious self needs in order to feel better. It is about caring for yourself.

My own definition of anxiety that I have come up with when talking to my children is that it is when you do not quite feel safe in your life. You are constantly trying to find ways to feel safer. If that is you, if rather than sometimes feeling anxious you actually have anxiety, you do not ever quite feel safe in your life and you are constantly trying to find ways to feel safer, it can be a real challenge. I am not minimising that at all. You never quite feel safe and then you need to push yourself to do something new or push out of your comfort zone or push to reach a goal, and trying to manage the feeling of not being safe is exhausting.

As with everything, though, this is why I bang on about being excessively kind to ourselves. You can make yourself feel safe. Your unconscious mind does not give a damn whether you are having a scary meeting or writing a book or doing whatever on earth it is that is freaking you out, the smallest thing or the biggest thing, it doesn't actually care. All your unconscious mind wants is to feel safe. So if you wrap it up, as in wrapping yourself up in a duvet and having a little cry, letting out some of that stress and talking to yourself in a kind way, having a warm drink and a nap, it will feel safe. It does not care that you still have to have the meeting; it is not bothered. You have made it feel safe, and then everything else becomes something that you can deal with.

We all have different experiences of not feeling safe, and I am still working on it as I still do not always catch it quickly enough to stop the panic from happening. When I do not feel safe because I put myself out there or said yes to something or agreed to the next challenge, what happens then is that my unconscious mind tells me everything that I need to do. So my thoughts start to spiral, and I think that I need to have a better handle on my finances and eat more healthily and have a better work-life balance but also to do a better job of marketing my business, and I could be a better friend, but I could also be providing a better service to my clients, I need to make more money and improve my website ... A lot of those things are probably true, there are probably improvements I can make, there are things I can learn and things I can change, new tools I can use, but the point is that these are ongoing things throughout my life. I can choose when and how to improve any of those things. What happens, though, when I do not feel safe is that my unconscious mind decides that all of those things are now completely essential, right at this moment. They are all equally urgent and essential for my safety, so of course I become completely overwhelmed because I cannot do anything about most of them in the moment, and I certainly cannot deal with them all at once or deal with them when I am terrified and overwhelmed.

That spiral when suddenly nothing feels safe and

everything feels like a huge problem, despite people telling you that it is not? The answer is to make yourself feel safe. Give your unconscious mind the safety that it needs without trying to fix anything. It is what you do in that moment. Sometimes we need exercise, sometimes we need a nap, sometimes we need a hug or a glass of wine with a friend. We need to find that safety and then, when we have it, we can do the thing that we have already agreed to, and we can look honestly at whether there are things that we could be working on or changing, but we need that emotional safety first.

For some of us this is going to involve more than just a cuddle up with a cuppa. This could involve some therapy or some counselling or some coaching, taking a step to really dig into where some of these fears are coming from and finding ways to tackle them long term. If you have never looked into this and where your anxiety is coming from, there could be a bigger piece of work here. No matter how you deal with the fears, though, they are a separate beast to be tamed. They are real and they need to be handled, but they are not allowed to have a say in your choices.

Mindset Block Alert!

My fear stops me from doing things
I know I want to do.

Still do the things anyway no matter how you deal with the fears; do the things anyway that are going to get you to where you need to be.

Fear is not allowed to stop you from reaching your goals. Do not put the fear in the driving seat. It can be a really annoying passenger, sometimes it will be in charge of the radio, irritating you to death, but never let it drive.

What is the next step you need to take to get to where you want to be? Are you feeling the fear? That is normal. Do it anyway. Do it today, and then manage the fear when you are already on the path. The fear is not going to go anywhere; you are always going to have that bag of anxiety, even though the size of it will change. It can be managed. Feel the fear and do it anyway ... and then after the doing, be excessively kind to yourself and that is how we squeeze every last drop of enjoyment out of life.

Thinking Points

- ♀ Recognise what you need in order to feel safe.
- ♀ Do some things that scare you if they will get you closer to your goals.
- ♀ Once you have done the scary thing, show yourself excessive kindness and make yourself feel safe again.
- ♀ Your fears are real and cannot be squashed, they can only be soothed.
- ♀ Give your fears a fair hearing, but never let them in the driving seat.

OTHER PEOPLE'S FEARS

We have talked about our own fears and anxiety, but how do other people's fears and anxiety make a difference in our world? How can we recognise that?

Have you heard the phrase 'crab bucket'? I came across it in a Terry Pratchett novel – I am a huge Terry Pratchett fan – and it struck me as a really recognisable phenomenon, and I discovered it is a widely recognised idea, 'the crab mentality'. Apparently, if you collect crabs at the beach and put them in a bucket ready to cook them, you don't need to put a lid on the bucket. The crabs will not escape. Why not? Well, if any crab tries to climb out of the bucket, the other crabs will grab onto it and pull it back down. The crabs actually keep themselves in captivity; they don't need anyone else to stop them from climbing to freedom.

Does this sound familiar? At many times in our lives we can find ourselves living in a crab bucket. Perhaps members of our family tend to think of themselves as not able to do certain things or not deserving of certain things, and they try to give us those same beliefs. That's a crab bucket. Perhaps our friends are all at a certain stage of life or in certain circumstances, and they're happy as long as we don't want to do things differently. That's a crab bucket. Perhaps our community is structured in a way to keep us small. Perhaps it is a wider issue depending on the community or culture or society we find ourselves in.

So how can we spot this crab bucket mentality? Some of these are tell-tale phrases, have you heard any of these?

* 'Yeah, but no one likes their job, do they?'
* 'I know, but all men are like that.'
* 'I just don't understand why you would want to do that!'
* 'No, that's not for the likes of us.'
* 'Yeah, but that's just what marriage is like, though, isn't it?'
* 'Ooh, you are brave to do that!'

Do any of these sound familiar?

Often this whole mentality is rooted in the fear of not belonging and the fear of having to change. If you are part of a group of people who all have similar problems, it can feel really cosy and safe to complain about them together, and even though the problems remain, at least you all feel as though you belong. If you are in a group of friends and everyone is having a whinge about their husbands, or if you are in a group of people and everybody hates their job, or everyone is struggling with a similar issue and that is what has brought you together, it just feels lovely and safe. You all belong together, but what is binding you is a joint misery.

When a member of the group tries to move forward to a

solution or tries to do something new, that can give everyone else in the group the fear that perhaps the gang will break up. Perhaps they as an individual will get left behind if they don't want a solution or they are not ready for a change. You'll have heard the phrase 'misery loves company', and it is true. People may not want you to change, to grow, to improve, to develop and become happier, not because they are terrible people but because it scares them. They may get left behind without any company in their misery, and they may not feel able to join you in moving forwards.

The fear of having to change is a big one that drives this crab bucket mentality. For example, if it turns out that not all marriages are unhappy, if that is not actually true, the people who imagine that 'this is just what marriage is like' will have to confront the fact that **they** are unhappy and that is not the norm. That is really scary. They are likely to be terrified of the choices they would have to make and the things they would have to face in order to change that situation. So they, no doubt unconsciously, choose to persuade others that being miserable in a marriage and not having their needs met is just the normal way of the world. Everyone belongs together in their dissatisfaction and nobody is going to get left behind.

This is not malicious. This is rarely a conscious choice. It is the way people behave because they are frightened of what it would mean if it turns out their situation is not just what everybody in the world accepts. It is really important to be able to recognise it, though, because when you see it for what it is, you can make your own choices. You can choose to belong to a different group of people or to counterbalance the crabs in your life by spending time with people who build you up and cheer you on.

Mindset Block Alert!

Other people changing and growing scares me.

Or

I want to grow and change but other people's fears are holding me back.

Getting curious can really help. If someone close to you is anxious about you growing and changing, ask them what it is they fear. Putting the focus onto their fears rather than your decisions can be helpful to both of you, and it can lead to a useful conversation, rather than a confrontation about whether what you are doing is right or wrong. Fear makes people angry, so if they are scared for you or scared for themselves, and you are scared of not having their support, it ends up in a row. Whereas if you have a curious conversation about what it is they are scared of, what they are worried is going to happen, that can be a lot more productive.

People are usually trying to keep you safe, often by employing the same tactics which they use to keep themselves safe, which are stay small, don't take up space, don't get noticed. If that is their tactic and it feels like it has worked for them, they are going to try to keep you safe in the same way. If you have decided against that approach because you know it is not serving you, recognise they are advocating it from a place of love but also fear. You can be grateful for the fact that they love you, and you can be compassionate towards their fears for themselves and for you, but you don't need to make those things a part of your decision making. It is their choice to stay small, not take up space, not get noticed. That might serve them – it probably doesn't – and that is up to them. We can understand it is what they think is safe, but we know their approach will not serve us and we want something else.

When I have done things that other people see as risky or brave or 'out there', often people think that I cannot see the risks. They feel the need to point out the risks and the 'what ifs' because they imagine I haven't seen those issues. Perhaps they are not used to taking risks; they imagine that if I am taking a risk it must be because I haven't spotted that it's risky, so they are trying to keep me safe by pointing out the potential problems. In actual fact, what has, of course, happened is that I have seen the risks and am well aware of them, and they are risks that I have decided I am comfortable in taking. For a lot of people that is such a different approach – that you would see a risk and be comfortable in taking it – so they think that I just must not have seen what the risks are.

Life is actually all risk. We do a thing, it's risky. We choose not to do a thing, that's risky. We risk something every time we step out of the door, and every time we stay in. It is all risk. Every day we are calculating which risks we are comfortable with taking, but those of us who push ourselves a little bit are quite happy in taking certain risks or happy in feeling the fear and doing it anyway, which I discussed earlier in the book.

Sometimes it can be helpful to explain to others (if we feel the need to justify ourselves, which we don't have to) that we have seen the risks, and we are comfortable with taking them. We see the risks as worthwhile and less of a problem than choosing not to do the thing and missing out as a consequence. Staying small feels like more of a risk to me than the risks inherent in growing and changing.

So if you do find someone hanging on to your leg, trying to pull you back down into the bucket, think about how you can put in place some boundaries with that person. It depends who they are: sometimes you can do that with love, sometimes you need to do that with a fairly firm hand, depending on the relationship. You do need boundaries in place, though, because them consistently trying to pull you down when you want to move up is really unhelpful and pretty unfair, even though we understand where their actions are coming from. If they do love you and want to express love for you, it needs to be done in a different way that actually serves you.

They might never climb up. It might be that you do actually have to leave them behind; you may have to fulfil that fear they have. That is their choice. No matter what they think to be true, they have the same choice that you do. They can stay where they are or they can move up and on and change. It is their choice if they get left behind. Your choice, the thing you are in control of, is whether you want to see over the lip of the bucket and see the big wide world beyond. I am telling you now, there is a whole lot more of life to enjoy outside the bucket. I highly advocate climbing out of it and kicking away anyone trying to hold you down! Outside the bucket is where it's at.

Thinking Points

- Other people will try to keep you small because of their own fears.
- You can recognise their good intentions and still have boundaries in place with them.
- You have the choice to leave those fears behind and live the life you want.
- Who in your life is holding you back because they are scared?

TAKING UP SPACE

I f you are a fan of Glennon Doyle, as I am, you will be familiar with the phrase 'taking up space'. I am not going to be talking about it in exactly the same way that she does: I am going to be looking at a particular aspect of it, which is why we sometimes stay small, why we don't take up space, and how the people in our lives around us can help or hinder us with that.

Let's start by looking at something you may or may not have already come across: the drama triangle, as first described by Stephen Karpman.

PERPETRATOR
'It's All Your Fault'
Sets strict limits unnecessarily • Blames • Criticises • Keeps Victim
oppressed • Is mobilised by anger • Rigid, authoritative stance •
'Critical' parent.

VICTIM
'Poor Me'
Feels victimised, oppressed, helpless, hopeless, powerless,
ashamed • Looks for a Rescuer who will perpetuate their negative
feelings • If stays in Victim position, will block self from making
decisions, solving problems, pleasure and self-understanding •
'Dejected' stance.

RESCUER
'Let Me Help You'
Rescues when really doesn't want to • Feels guilty if doesn't rescue • Keeps Victim dependent • Gives permission to fail • Expects to fail in rescue attempts.

The Perpetrator/Victim/Rescuer Triangle

PERPETRATOR
Blames & Abuses
"you are the problem"
"what is wrong with you?"

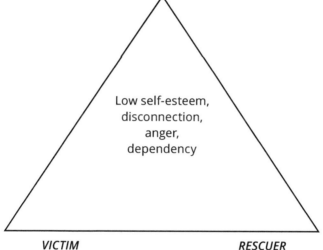

Low self-esteem,
disconnection,
anger,
dependency

VICTIM *Placates & Gets Abused* "you are always doing this to me" "I deserve this" "I am helpless"	**RESCUER** *Co-behaves, Enables, Fixes* "I must fix this" "I am the solution"

Source: relate.org.uk

This concept helps us to understand types of behaviour, and all of us will engage in all of those behaviours at one time or another. We will recognise ourselves in all of those 'types'.

We are not talking here about 'victim blaming' or suggesting that all of the things that have happened to you are your fault; we are talking about a specific way of creating and maintaining drama, and we are using the word 'victim' in the sense as outlined above. The victim in this definition finds it in some ways helpful or pleasant (or maybe just familiar) to be needy and wait for someone else to fix it, to sort it all out for them. The problem is all somebody else's fault and the victim cannot be the strong one. Not in instances where a person genuinely needs help, that is a very different thing, but in instances where a person does have the resources and capabilities to help themselves, but chooses not to and prefers to be seen as needing help.

Then there is the rescuer. This is one I am sure we will all recognise, we will have done this ourselves. Somebody needs something, somebody has a problem, and it is so juicy to be the rescuer. We are going to be the person to fix it all for them, to sort it all out, we have the answers, we are going to be amazing! A rescuer loves a victim and a victim loves a rescuer. This is the dynamic that I want to focus on in this chapter as I think it is a pattern that a lot of people fall into for totally understandable reasons, but it can keep us very small.

It is a vulnerable position to be in if you are in a relationship where you tend to be the one who doesn't have a huge amount of agency, or you are the one who doesn't have a huge amount of confidence. You don't really feel like you are good enough, you can't do the things, you are not as good as other people and everything is difficult. You do not feel like you are capable, and the rescuer in the relationship is perfectly happy with that because oh my goodness they are ready to do it all for you so you don't have to worry about a thing. That feels very comfortable and wonderful because you don't have to do anything or grow or challenge yourself, except it makes both of you vulnerable. As the victim, you are vulnerable because the smaller you make your life the more scared you become. Let's say you are scared of leaving the house, therefore you stay in all the time. That is not going to take the fear away. What is likely to happen is, because you haven't done anything to build up your confidence or address the fear, it is probably going to get worse. The smaller you make your life, the smaller it becomes, and I have seen this with people I know personally where people have allowed their fears to take over and have been encouraged in that by a rescuer who has the best of intentions. The rescuer says, 'Don't worry, you don't have to do anything. I'll do this for you', and the victim gets smaller and smaller and smaller.

The rescuer is vulnerable as well. These are not bad people: these are often people who love us dearly, and what happens is one day the victim finds their strength. We see this so often when women become mothers; it is such a transformational experience that if you weren't confident before or you felt small before or not good enough, when you become a mother eventually the experience shows you your strength. Then you become someone who wants to grow and change and challenge yourself, and suddenly the rescuer is no longer an appropriate person to have in your life. They have left themselves vulnerable to being left behind because the dynamic you have set up together is keeping you small.

Having someone in your life who keeps you small and tries to help you by allowing you to not face anything is not helpful. Neither is having a perpetrator in your life who blames and criticises all the time. Guess what is helpful? Yep, it's that ol' excessive kindness again. Excessive kindness, but real kindness, not keeping you small. Kindly supporting and gently encouraging.

Managing anxiety, as we have discussed, is really helpful too, it is all part of it. It is important to be with people who want to support us to grow. Not bully us into growth, not keep us away from growth in case it hurts us, but support us to grow. Not belittle us but believe in us.

You may have seen this quote which has done the rounds of the internet pinboards:

To love someone is to remind them of how wonderful they are when they have forgotten.

That is central to my message here. We want to be around people who remind us what we are capable of and how much potential we have when we have forgotten or when we are in fear.

I have struggled with this mindset block myself. If I don't have any problems or if I don't have needs or if I am not struggling or crying or stressing or telling people how awful things are, maybe people are going to ignore me. Nobody is going to come to help me and I will be all alone.

 Mindset Block Alert!

I am really scared that if I get my shit together nobody will look after me.

The reality is, in my experience, people will always support you and be there for you because they love you and you have worth. They are likely to support you more, in fact, if you are not in a victim mentality because they will know you can handle things, so supporting you is not going to leave them overexposed. By which I mean if they encourage you to talk to them about things that are bothering you, you are not going to text them every night for three weeks with all of your problems, expecting them to rescue you. You are going to give them some stuff to help you with, and then when they say they have to go and do something else and talk to you later, you are not going to fall apart.

However, if your value to someone is only in how needy you are, then they are a rescuer and that dynamic is an unhealthy one.

As we discussed in the last chapter, our growth can be intimidating to some people. A healthy relationship is one where both people can handle their own shit and they *choose* to be vulnerable with each other, open up and share their challenges and support each other. They do not *have* to do that. It is an equal two-way street, where each person supports the other through their struggles, it is not always the same one-way dynamic.

Some people really want to support us, but they don't know how. Not everybody who is sitting in the rescuer seat wants to be there, but perhaps they don't know any other way to help. Some people are natural 'fixers' and they see fear or emotion as something they need to change – they must take away the fear or stop the tears. If you are with people like that, the key is to explain what you need. Have an open conversation. Tell them what you would like to achieve with their support. Tell them how they will know when you just need help and encouragement and when you actually want to quit. Important point here: quitting or keeping going with any growth activity is your responsibility. Never say to somebody, 'You have to make me give up smoking' or 'You have to stop me from eating the extra thousand calories'. You have to choose to do those things. The person supporting you can encourage you, and if you say, 'I really want to keep going but it is really hard today', they can cheer you on. If you say, 'I am done with this', it is their job to say, 'Fine, okay'. It is not their responsibility. Tell them that you want their encouragement and support until such time as you decide to quit, and if you are going to give up on your goal, it is not their responsibility to push you back into it.

What should they do if you are scared or upset? Tell them! If they are a fixer but you do not want fixing, you want to be listened to or encouraged or reminded of how awesome you are, tell them what it is they need to do in those situations.

Also, what qualities in you would you like them to recognise and celebrate? We all have those things that we like about ourselves or that we want to grow more of in ourselves, and they are the things that we are desperate for approval about from the people in our lives. So tell your people about those things. They are not mind-readers, and they have their own things they think are awesome about you, and it is great to hear about those, but tell them if there is something you would really love for them to recognise and encourage in you. If they love you, they will welcome that information. You can ask them these same questions to find out from them how they want to be supported.

A healthy relationship – friendship, intimate relationship, parent-child relationship – is one where you encourage each other to take up space. Nobody is trying to keep anybody small. Nobody is scared of growth. If you feel that one of your relationships is an unhealthy one where somebody is doing all the rescuing of someone who is comfortable as a victim, it is probably the case that you need to make some changes.

The more space you take up, the more confident you will feel. Keep small, and you will get smaller. Start to grow, and you will get bigger.

Thinking Points

💡 A relationship between a rescuer and a victim is vulnerable for both parties, and holds back each individual from reaching their full potential.

- ⚲ We want to be around people who remind us what we are capable of and how much potential we have when we have forgotten or when we are in fear.
- ⚲ A healthy relationship, friendship, intimate relationship, parent-child relationship is one where you encourage each other to take up space.
- ⚲ Keep small, and you will get smaller.

MONEY

So we come to our final topic, and this is possibly the most anxiety-provoking subject of them all. Does the idea of making money or dealing with money make you uncomfortable? Do you say things like, 'I just want to help people' and 'I hate putting up my prices'? Do you know that you are not charging what you are worth, but you can't seem to do anything about it?

Money mindset is a big issue for the self-employed, particularly amongst women, so you are not alone. The first thing I will say is that I highly recommend Denise Duffield-Thomas's book *Get Rich, Lucky Bitch* – don't be put off by the title, it is an excellent book, definitely a game-changer, and it will make things easier.

In the meantime, let's have some quick thoughts on what we can do to make money a little less scary, and a little bit less of a problem.

Look full in the face the fact that money panics you. That is nothing to be ashamed of, it doesn't mean anything, apart from that it is something that needs to go on your list of stuff to work through.

Let's try to get a bit clearer on what the problem might be. Grab a piece of paper, and answer these questions, and please be as honest as you can – no one will see your answers.

* What does a rich person look like?
* How does a rich person act?
* People who want to make money are...
* Having more money than I need to live on would be...
* People who don't have much money are...
* If I want to be rich, that means...

Chances are you have just written down loads of value judgements about yourself and other people which are purely based on the number in their bank account and whether they would like to have more money than they need. Be clear about the judgements you are making and the beliefs you are carrying around. None of what you have written is concrete truth, but what you have written reveals the stories that you are taking with you through life about money and income, wanting money, having it, and it is important to be clear about that because some of those beliefs might well be holding you back and not serving you.

What are the money stories that you grew up with? So much of our attitude towards money comes from our childhood, either our experiences of having money or not, or what our families told us about money, how they acted about money, their own money mindset. Get clear on what those stories are – what are the rules you were given, consciously or unconsciously, about money?

Money, currency, finance all came about because bartering was inconvenient. You *could* give me food that you have grown in your garden in exchange for a coaching session with me, but I think we can all see the flaws inherent in that. It is hard to make that work, and so we have money. Money is a way of getting what we want and what we need in exchange for the skills that we have, or it is a way of other people giving us what we want and what we need via the skills that they have. We all fulfil our own needs and wants or we fulfil each others', and the money moves around. That's it. Everything else is a story or a judgement or an unconscious rule.

So what are these 'shoulds' about money that you have in this little sack of thoughts that you carry around with you? Are they serving you? It is important to look at them, own them, understand them so you can decide whether you want to change them.

I have money stories – I have many, we all do. My main story about money is that money is freedom. I can do more of what I want, including helping other people, the more money I have. That is not a fact or a truth, it is just my story, that is how I view money. How about you?

Money causes more stress than almost anything else. We all need it and to engage with it in some way, and yet we have so many beliefs and stories and rules around it that just engaging with it at all can be hugely stressful. We can worry very much about changes in our income – having more or having less. Often we are on a knife edge of anxiety worrying that something could be taken away at any moment, or worrying if unexpected money comes in. We hear about people who get a windfall, inherit money, somehow suddenly get 'extra' and they very quickly spend it. They get rid of it as quickly as possible because it makes them so uncomfortable. Money issues don't always manifest as never spending anything. It could be that you spend all the time. It is all about the stories and whether we feel safe with or without money.

When we are thinking about taking an income from our business, here is what we need to focus on. Firstly, how much money do we need? Answering that question requires doing some budgeting, and all I mean by that is going through our bank accounts and writing down what comes out every month without fail. The mortgage, the utilities, the petrol, the food bill, the council tax … the stuff that is always going to come out. How much money do we need to cover all of that before we even think about the fun things we want to do?

If we had more money, what would we do with it? If having more money is a scary thought, you might want to shy away from this question, but if you did have more money, it would, of course, be completely under your control what you did with that. You could save it, spend it, give it to charity, bury it in the garden, roll around on the bed in it – you can do whatever you want with your own money! On the basis that there are no rules and no 'shoulds', what would you actually do with it if you had some more?

How could your life be improved if you had a higher income? That is so subjective – when we talk about money, we think *new car, new house, new clothes*; we think about the stuff we could buy, which is fine, that might be the answer for you. If you had a higher income, your life would be improved because you could have more of the stuff you want. That is just one option, though, there are loads of other ways that money can improve the quality of our lives. It might give us more opportunities for self-care. It might give us more opportunities to see the people we love, especially if we have friends and family a long way away or abroad. It might give us more opportunities for healthcare. It might give us different choices. It might give us the opportunity to enrich our lives by giving more to charity. There are numerous ways more money could improve our lives, and only you can answer how it could improve your life because only you know what 'improve' means for you.

A couple more questions for those of us who are business owners. Firstly, what will potential customers think if our prices are too low? I can't think of many areas in my life where the cheapest product is what I'll go for, because my value judgement, my story, is that cheap means badly made, likely to break, not up to scratch, not as good as other options, not of value. That is my story, it is not 'the truth', but we have to bear in mind that if our prices are too low, or lower than everyone else's, there's a decent chance that potential customers might see us as not very good. There are reasons to keep your prices at a certain level, besides the idea of your making more money. There is a value perception that goes with our prices.

Secondly, whose decision is it to buy our products or services? Of course it is the client's decision, isn't it? We are not conning anyone; we are not duping anyone; we are not taking advantage of anyone. We are stating what we offer and how much it is, and other people will make a decision whether or not to spend their money on it. We accept that decision and we say, 'Thank you for your business'. So there is no need for us to worry about other people having to spend X amount of money on our services. It is not our responsibility to manage their money for them.

As an aside, if you struggle with how much money to take from your business, I can highly recommend the Profit First system which my accountant advocates, as do many others. Look it up – it is a straightforward, easy-to-understand and easy-to-manage system for knowing how much to pay yourself, how much to put aside for tax and how much to keep in your business.

If you want to make a bit of progress on the ol' money mindset, then start this chapter again and work through the questions I have posed and look up the resources I have suggested. Get clear on what is serving you and what attitudes you may need to change. In the meantime, head over to a mirror, take a good look at yourself, in your sweatpants or your jeans, with your messy hair and dodgy skin and everything you don't like about the way you look, blah blah blah. What you see in the mirror right now is what a wealthy person looks like. All those judgements you make, actually, there is no reason a wealthy person can't look like exactly what you see in the mirror. If you ever are wealthy, or just financially comfortable or whatever it is you are aiming for, you will still be and will always be you. It is not going to mean that you become a different person.

Money can help us, though, to squeeze every last drop of enjoyment out of life.

Thinking Points

- Can you be honest about how anxious money makes you?
- What judgements are you making about people who have, or do not have, money?
- What are your 'money stories'?
- It is your clients' responsibility what they choose to spend their money on – not yours.
- Having more or less money will not make you a different person – but money can give you more choices.

CONCLUSION

As much as I hope this book has given you lots of answers and insights, I hope it has also left you with many questions. Life is about recognising the questions we need to ask ourselves, and getting clear on our answers, or even just getting clear on our feelings about the questions. That is never easy, but being excessively kind to ourselves through that process makes it far more likely that we will make some progress.

You are who you are. You have the same worth as everyone else. You do not need to apologise for being you. You do not need to take up less space than anybody else. You deserve to make money from the skills and interests that you have, and you can reach your goals if you show up and keep talking about what you can offer to people and how you can help them. Nothing about being successful in business is easy, but neither does it have to be mind-crushingly hard. Hold your own hand, be gentle with yourself, and you will find that your confidence grows each time you ease yourself through a challenge with kindness and self-forgiveness.

I said at the start that I do not believe in quick and easy systems, but there is one mantra that has served me well and which can help us to find the calm when the overwhelm threatens. That is: breathe, bathroom, beverage. No matter how much stress you are under, you always have time to take a deep breath, have a wee and grab a drink. You will feel like you don't have the time because adrenaline makes you seize up, but that's why we take the deep breath first. One big deep breath reduces the adrenaline.

Once the adrenaline has reduced, you can have a wee and grab a drink, and then you will be in a much better position to deal with whatever crisis is afoot. Having a full bladder, being dehydrated and with shallow breathing is a recipe for meltdown. So keep this reminder handy – it really does help.

That is only a very quick fix, though, for moments of rising panic. For longer-term results and happiness, it is those pesky mindset blocks that we have to identify and figure out, being compassionate towards ourselves along the way.

None of us will make it to where we want to be if we wait for somebody else to give us permission. There are no rules to which we have to adhere (apart from the laws of the land). Anything that you think of as a rule was a suggestion put in place to make somebody else's life easier, or advice from someone who cared about you in their attempt to keep you safe. You can choose how much of that is still serving you, and ditch the rest. Show up for yourself every day, and love yourself the way you want and deserve to be loved. Success, money, respect, achievement, fulfilment, whatever it is that you desire, will come to you far more easily if you do that one thing. It is the only thing I would say needs to be consistent: love for yourself. No bullshit, it really is the key to happiness.

ACKNOWLEDGEMENTS

I have needed a fair bit of support and encouragement to get this book to publication. To get to a point in my life where I have something meaningful to say I have needed even more.

For getting this book across the finish line, I would like to thank:

* Lisa Curtis of LVC Projects for producing my podcast.
* Melanie Cotton of Argentum Proofreading for proof-reading my drafts and providing invaluable advice.
* Catherine Williams of Chapter One Book Production for typesetting the book and providing more invaluable advice.
* Vicky Murray of VCM Graphic Design for my beautiful cover artwork.
* my mum who did an initial proofread to ensure I wasn't embarrassing myself.

For getting me to the age of 42 with the clarity and confidence to make this book a reality, I would like to thank:

* My parents, Fiona and Peter, who taught me much of what is in this book.
* Lucy Ruddle IBCLC for teaching me how to listen – to others and to myself.
* Beth Penfold, The Change Coach, for coaching me through my demons.
* Caroline Boardman, Caroline Boardman Consulting, for joining me in building a community of fantastic business owners.
* My team at Clear Day – Kirsten, Angie, Elaina, Emmeline, Jo, Laura, Linda, Mel, Sam and Vic – who do all the work and keep me sane.
* My clients who have taught me so much.
* Jenny Cooper, Jennifer Cooper Timesaver, for being president of my fan club since we were eight years old.
* Alex Siegling, who has dramatically reduced the bullshit and increased the happiness in my life.

I couldn't have done it without you all.